◆

READ UP

VOLUME 1

GET THE
CONVERSATION
STARTED

◆

BOOK SELECTIONS
& QUESTIONS FOR
READING GROUPS

InterVarsity Press
Heart. Soul. Mind. Strength.

InterVarsity Press
P.O. Box 1400, Downers Grove, IL 60515-1426
World Wide Web: www.ivpress.com
Email: email@ivpress.com

InterVarsity Press® is the book-publishing division of InterVarsity
Christian Fellowship/USA®, a movement of students and faculty active
on campus at hundreds of universities, colleges and schools of nursing in
the United States of America, and a member movement of the International Fellowship of Evangelical Students. For information about local
and regional activities, write Public Relations Dept., InterVarsity
Christian Fellowship/USA, 6400 Schroeder Rd., P.O. Box 7895, Madison,
WI 53707-7895, or visit the IVCF website at www.intervarsity.org.

Cover design: David Fassett
Interior design: Beth Hagenberg
Images: *Woman with coffee:* © *Ryan Lane/iStockphoto*

ISBN 978-0-8308-5812-5 (print)
ISBN 978-0-8308-5997-9 (digital)

Printed in the United States of America ∞

g green
press
INITIATIVE
InterVarsity Press is committed to protecting the environment
and to the responsible use of natural resources. As a member
of Green Press Initiative we use recycled paper whenever possible. To
learn more about the Green Press Initiative, visit www.greenpressini-
tiative.org.

P 15 14 13 12 11 10 9 8 7 6 5 4 3 2 1
Y 22 21 20 19 18 17 16 15 14

Dear Fellow Reader:

Reading is a solitary act. For many of us it is a form of retreat—a welcomed silence and deserved rest from our demanding routines. We have our favorite spot in the house: the unmade bed, the couch long enough to doze on, or maybe the off-limits living room. Wherever it is, when we are there with book in hand and maybe our favorite cup of tea (my favorite is anything peach) all who encounter us know to "shush." It's reading time.

But, when you read a really good book, aren't you just dying to talk about it? Halfway through or maybe even in the introduction, who comes to mind? There's always someone we can't wait to share our newfound knowledge with, or tell of our disbelief of an author's opinion. We can agree or disagree with the author, and he or she is none the wiser. But our dear fellow reader is always eager to hear our perspective. Or at least we hope so.

In reading groups we don't have to hope someone wants to hear our opinions —it's expected! And even better, the idea or concept that we missed in our reading is often what our fellow readers will discover and share with us. Our "aha" moments are multiplied in conversation. Even in disagreement— maybe especially when we disagree—there is opportunity to learn from one another as we seek to understand different points of view.

In the end, our shared conversation becomes another welcomed respite as we glean wisdom and receive understanding from one another. My hope is that the diverse assortment of titles in this first volume of Read Up *will provide you and your group with books that lead to both stimulating reading and meaningful conversation.*

Read up!

Lorraine Caulton
Editor, *Read Up*

P.S. Visit ivpress.com/readup to view our new Reading Group page.

CONTENTS

"You can never get a cup of tea large enough
or a book long enough to suit me."

C. S. LEWIS

BIRMINGHAM REVOLUTION
Martin Luther King Jr.'s Epic Challenge to the Church

Edward Gilbreath

Dr. Martin Luther King Jr.'s words and historic efforts as the Moses of this civil rights movement stand out as perhaps the most significant instance of a modern Christian leader acting in a prophetic role to instigate political change. In many ways "The Letter from Birmingham Jail" stands at the center of that movement. In this book African American journalist Edward Gilbreath explores the place of that letter in the life and work of Dr. King.

Birmingham Revolution is not simply a work of historical reflection. Gilbreath encourages us to reflect on the relevance of King's work for the church and culture of our day. Whether it's in debates about immigration, economic redistribution or presidential birth certificates, race continues to play a role in shaping society. What part will the church play in the ongoing struggle?

> *"The calling of a prophet is a glorious burden. The prophetic voice of Martin Luther King is as needed by the church today as it was half a century ago. Edward Gilbreath allows us to hear it with depth and power."*
>
> John Ortberg, senior pastor of Menlo Park Presbyterian Church and author of *Who Is This Man?*

ABOUT THE AUTHOR: Edward Gilbreath is the author of *Reconciliation Blues: A Black Evangelical's Inside View of White Christianity*. An award-winning journalist, he serves as an editor at large for *Christianity Today* magazine and as the executive director of communications for the Evangelical Covenant Church.

INTERVARSITY PRESS

◆ QUESTIONS

1. On page 12, Gilbreath asserts that "the idea of race is so entrenched in our thinking that it's almost impossible to imagine not seeing the world through a racialized lens." Do you agree? Why or why not?

2. According to one Christian leader, Martin Luther King Jr.'s "Letter from Birmingham Jail" suggests that the fight for social justice is "an essential mark of the gospel" (p. 17). How does the idea of justice fit into your understanding of the Christian gospel?

3. Chapter 2 features fourteen key themes and experiences that shaped Martin Luther King Jr.'s early life. Which one surprised you the most?

4. In chapter 3 pastor Robert Graetz said the civil rights movement was a church movement (pp. 50-51). Do you think people overlook this fact? What would the movement have looked like without the involvement of the church?

5. The circumstances that preceded Dr. King's arrest in Birmingham on Good Friday almost derailed the movement. According to King, he had to "make a faith act" (p. 70). What do the events in room 30 of the Gaston Motel tell us about King's understanding of faith?

6. According to one scholar, "Letter from Birmingham Jail" represented "a culmination of all of King's ideas, theology, experiences, and civil rights tactics" (p. 107). How do you see all of these things coming to bear in King's letter?

7. Chapter 11 explores how our perceptions of Dr. King have become distorted over the years. Before reading this book, what was your perception of King? What is it now?

8. Birmingham native Diane McWhorter observes that many Birminghamians have tried to go from "amnesia" to "closure" regarding their city's history (p. 155). "You can't go around it," she says. "You must go through it." What does it mean to "go through" our difficult history?

9. In the epilogue (pp. 167-69), Gilbreath offers four concluding ideas about Dr. King and the Birmingham revolution: (1) know where your power comes from, (2) embrace your inner Shuttlesworth, (3) let no man despise your youth, (4) live your letter. What might these ideas look like in your personal faith journey?

Countless books and articles have been written about Martin Luther King Jr. over the years. What inspired you to share another perspective on King in *Birmingham Revolution*?

Edward Gilbreath: There's a multitude of books about King and the civil rights movement, but I felt compelled to tell the story from the perspective of an African American evangelical who was born a year after Dr. King's death. Many people from my generation and younger don't always have a full picture of who King really was—his courage, his radicalism, his faith, his humanity. I wanted to shed light on these aspects of King and, above all, show the church that everything he did was driven by his Christian faith and values.

What was significant about Birmingham as a stage for the civil rights movement?

Edward: In 1963 Birmingham, Alabama, was one of the most notorious strongholds of segregation and white supremacy in the South. It was a place described by King as "the most thoroughly segregated city in the United States." Not only were the public institutions, such as libraries, segregated but it was so severe that even books that contained photos of black rabbits and white rabbits together were banned from the library shelves. It was a city where bullets, bombs and burning crosses served as constant deterrents to blacks who aspired to anything greater than their assigned station of inequality. Rev. Fred Shuttlesworth, a fiery Baptist preacher in Birmingham, had implored King and his Southern Christian Leadership Conference associates to come to Birmingham and help the city's black community confront segregation. He told them, "I assure you, if you come to Birmingham, we will not only gain prestige but really shake the country." He knew that if the movement could change things in Birmingham, it would reverberate throughout the nation.

What was the significance of King's "Letter from Birmingham"?

Edward: The Birmingham campaign started out slowly, but after King was arrested on Good Friday for his movement's public demonstration on the streets of Birmingham, things began to change. While in solitary confinement, he was shown a newspaper op-ed column by eight moderate clergymen in Birmingham. They implored him to wait for the laws to take effect. But King believed the black community had waited long enough; they needed to take a stand and stir the conscience of Birmingham and of the nation. His response to the op-ed was a passionate letter that spelled out the reasons why the movement couldn't wait and pointed out the differences between just and unjust laws. He wrote the letter on the margins of the newspaper, on scraps of any paper he could gather, and when he ran out, he reportedly wrote on the toilet paper in his cell. After its publication weeks later, the "Letter from Birmingham Jail" would become one of the most lucid and convincing arguments for social justice and civil rights that we've ever had. What's more, it was rooted in the theology and principles of the Christian gospel.

Why do you think King was more a "prophet" of social justice?

Edward: It's easy to want to write Dr. King off as just a leader who gave a good speech. But in doing that, we risk missing the fact that he was vehemently disliked in his day and that as time went on he was becoming increasingly angry and impatient with the pace of change in the nation. Late in his life he wrote, "Whites are not putting in a mass effort to re-educate themselves out of their racial ignorance." While he rejected the militancy of the Black Power movement, he understood the roots of its members' discontent. As a Christian minister and Nobel Peace Prize recipient, King also felt compelled to speak out against the Vietnam conflict. This also served to land him on some of America's "most hated" lists. In all these cases, he was speaking out as a prophet of social justice. But that's typically not the King that we choose to focus on today.

What do you hope readers take away from *Birmingham Revolution*?

Edward: I want people to discover the full humanity of Dr. Martin Luther King Jr., to move beyond viewing him as this gentle "I Have a Dream" character to seeing him as the prophetic and often radical Christian visionary that he was. I want people to discover and rediscover Dr. King's "Letter from Birmingham Jail" as a message encompassing his holistic vision of the gospel lived out in everyday life.

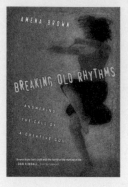

BREAKING OLD RHYTHMS

Answering the Call of a Creative God

Amena Brown

Foreword by Dan Kimball

Spoken word poet Amena Brown has made rhythm her life's work. In *Breaking Old Rhythms* she explores how we discover by rhythm both our God-given limitations and potential, and the ways we limit God's work in our lives. Read this book and be reminded, and encouraged, that while God has rhythm, God *is* love, and God's love carries us beyond our rhythms into a fuller, more fulfilling life.

"*Amena Brown is a gift—a breathtaking blend of poet, prophet and pioneer. Her life and words will bless your soul.*"

Margaret Feinberg, www.margaretfeinberg.com, author of *Scouting the Divine* and *Wonderstruck*

"*Amena Brown uses words to fill the soul like music. In* Breaking Old Rhythms *she creatively explores the idea that we all have a life rhythm, and that God is often found in the most unexpected places.*"

Michael Gungor, singer-songwriter

ABOUT THE AUTHOR: Amena Brown is a poet, speaker, journalist and event host from Atlanta, Georgia. The author of a chapbook and two spoken word CDs, Brown has performed and spoken at events across the nation, such as The RightNow Conference, Creativity World Forum, Catalyst Conference, Chick-fil-A Leadercast and the 2008 National Poetry Slam Competition, and has toured with Gungor.

Listen to a performance by Amena at ivpress.com/breakingoldrhythms.

INTERVARSITY PRESS

◆ QUESTIONS

1. The author's initial intent was to write a "how-to guide on what to do when you find yourself in a rut." The resulting idea, "breaking old rhythms," is a metaphor for being in a rut. What habits or ruts do you find yourself in today that you'd like to break?

2. The author's description of God as "old, beige, bald and with a really long goatee" (p.18) seemed unapproachable. How can our image of God impact our relationship to him?

3. How did the chapter "The Blessing of Irritation" help you view some of life's troubles differently? Are frustration and irritation motivators for you?

4. "If God is the DJ and my life is the dance floor, then he is in constant control of the songs that play" (p. 30). Is this a comforting or troubling statement to you? Why?

5. After a breakup Amena learns that letting go is a process. How can this understanding help us when breaking old rhythms?

6. In learning the waltz, Amena is told she is leading instead of following, which is necessary in formal dancing. She compares dancing and faith: "If faith is a dance, Jesus is always the lead" (p. 72). In what places in your life are you leading, when following is what is necessary?

7. To pray is to listen (p. 97). How does this challenge your approach to prayer?

8. Do the words *predictable, comfortable* and *convenient* make you feel safe and secure? What would it take for you to "think outside the box" as described in chapter 8?

9. We each carry "baggage." If your emotional baggage were physical baggage what would it look like?

10. Which poem in *Breaking Old Rhythms* was most meaningful to you?

What inspired you to write *Breaking Old Rhythms*?

Amena Brown: Broken rhythm has been a theme in my life and in my journey of faith. Everyone has experienced broken rhythm whether they could name it that or not. We've all experienced times when we thought our life was going one way and it took a drastic turn or when we were faced with a choice to either stick to what's comfortable or take a risk and do something different than what we imagined. I also wanted to write about how art, music and hip hop have informed my relationship with God. Wherever we are in our journey of faith, we all have a need to be closer to God. I wanted to write a book that talks about the experiences that help us grow closer to him, if we embrace them. *Breaking Old Rhythms* is derived from Bruce Lee's martial art principle "broken rhythm."

What is significant about that principle as it pertains to our lives?

Amena: In martial arts and boxing "broken rhythm" means using irregular rhythm to triumph over an opponent; by being unpredictable a fighter increases his chances of winning. In *Breaking Old Rhythms* I am using the principle of broken rhythm to apply to life and the journey of faith, to communicate how God uses the unpredictability of life to help us see him more clearly. Infusing these principles with lessons learned from dance, music, hip-hop culture, and stories of singleness and family, gives the book a distinct approach. *Breaking Old Rhythms* is not a guide or a how-to. Instead it takes a storytelling approach in hopes that the reader will find the beat of his or her own stories there and be encouraged to draw closer to God's rhythm in the process.

What was the most significant "broken rhythm" in your own life? What impact did that have on you?

Amena: One of my most significant "broken rhythm" experiences was leaving my corporate job to pursue writing, speaking and performing as a full-time job. I learned pretty quickly that being a full-time artist doesn't mean sitting at my laptop in my pajamas all day and writing when the mood hits me. Through breaking what was my 9 to 5 rhythm, I learned the importance of being an artist and an entrepreneur.

How and when did you become a spoken word artist?

Amena: I started performing poetry in speech competitions, but never my own poetry. I would perform Maya Angelou, James Weldon Johnson or Paul Robeson. My mom is the one who really encouraged me to perform my own work, so I did for the first time at seventeen years old and have been performing my own poetry ever since. I grew as a spoken word poet once I moved to Atlanta to attend Spelman College. Atlanta had and still has a thriving poetry scene, so I learned to sharpen my craft from watching so many great spoken word artists command the stage and take unique angles on different topics in their poems. My husband and I host a quarterly open mic in Atlanta. Being connected to the poetry scene still sharpens my writing and performance.

How does your work as an artist, particularly a poet, play into *Breaking Old Rhythms*?

Amena: As a poet, music and rhythms inspire me. I'm constantly looking to jazz, hip hop, film, storytelling and visual art for inspiration, and all of these things have unpredictable rhythm. In my search for inspiration, I have grown closer to God through experiences in the oddest of places, from a hip-hop club to a coffee house, in my cubicle and in the silence of my apartment. In order to write better and live more truly, I have realized it's necessary to break old rhythms often.

What do you hope readers take away from *Breaking Old Rhythms*?

Amena: Everyone has a rhythm, including God. If we are going to follow any rhythm, it should be his. God is a deejay, he mixes and masters everything that happens into our life and makes something beautiful of it (Romans 8:28). God can heal our broken hearts and use even painful experiences to bring us closer to him. We need stillness and silence to know God, and we should allow that to break our rhythm. Following Jesus is not a rote, mundane or monotonous experience. He shows us his rhythm and his beat and gives us the freedom to freestyle.

COFFEE WITH JESUS

David Wilkie

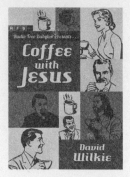

Thousands of people start every day with a shot of *Coffee with Jesus,* the enormously popular online comic strip. Here you'll enjoy classic entries and all-new, exclusive material, including twelve-panel megastrips and "behind the strip" reflections on life, faith and art.

"Like the first cup of the day, Coffee with Jesus *offers a much-needed jolt to our culturally captured versions of Christianity and some beloved sacred cows. Yup—including my own."*

Sean Gladding, author of *The Story of God, the Story of Us* **and** *Ten*

*"*Christianity Today, *the magazine I edited for twenty-eight years, was not known for its keen sense of humor. That's why* Coffee with Jesus *is one of my guilty pleasures. I read its sassy Jesus as a refuge from sober Christians and to make up for the smart-aleck gene missing from my DNA."*

David Neff, former editor in chief, *Christianity Today*

"I loved this book! I never use the phrase 'LOL'—I'm sorry, that's just how I was raised. But this book honestly had me laughing out loud."

Jon Acuff, *New York Times* **bestselling author of** *Start* **and** *Stuff Christians Like*

ABOUT THE AUTHOR: David Wilkie is the artist behind *Coffee with Jesus* and cofounder, with his wife, of Radio Free Babylon.

INTERVARSITY PRESS

◆ QUESTIONS

1. Wilkie writes, "The notion of Jesus sitting down for a cup of coffee with a bunch of very certain and opinionated people struck me as humorous" (p. 13). What topics are you "very certain and opinionated" about? What do you think Jesus would tease you about?

2. Which of the regular characters do you most closely identify with? Which are particularly hard for you to relate to? Why?

3. Satan is often depicted in art, literature and music. How does the depiction of Satan in *Coffee with Jesus* compare with other cultural depictions? What, in your mind, does *Coffee with Jesus* get right about Satan?

4. Does having Jesus pictured in every strip make it easier or harder for you to imagine your own conversations with him? Explain.

5. "Coffee Jesus" seems friendly, but he also regularly asserts his divine authority. Are you more comfortable with friendly Jesus or Jesus the authority figure? Why?

6. In the strip "About to Say" (p. 15), Jesus predicts that someday Lisa will be able to anticipate his words to her. What helps you anticipate what God might say to you in a given situation?

7. In the strip "Be Still" (p. 26), Lisa seems to be having an amazing experience with Jesus, even without words (or even because there are no words). What do you think is going on in their interaction?

8. Jesus seems to prefer flawed friends to perfect ones. Why do you think that is? How does that compare to your perception of Jesus?

9. Jesus often challenges the characters to learn, change, mature, grow up. Which of them is most likely to, do you think? Why? Where do you yourself fall on that spectrum?

10. Some people think comic strips are inherently too juvenile or shallow to learn anything significant from. How would you respond to those people? Explain.

11. If you had to propose a new "regular" for the strip, who would they be? What kind of person would make an interesting and funny addition to the cast of characters of *Coffee with Jesus*?

COURAGE AND CALLING

Embracing Your God-Given Potential

Gordon T. Smith

God calls us first to himself, to know and follow him, and also to a specific life purpose, a particular reason for being. This second call or "vocation" has implications not only for our work or occupation but also includes our giftedness, our weaknesses, our life in community and what we do day to day. In this book Gordon Smith invites you to discover your vocation by listening to God and becoming a coworker with him.

- What is my calling?
- How do I live it out in the midst of difficult relationships or moral challenges?
- Will my vocation change as I enter a new stage of life?

Smith addresses these questions and many more in the pages of this book. This new edition has been revised and updated throughout with two expanded chapters and a new chapter on four specific areas of calling.

Here is rich insight for all who long for the ears to hear and the courage to follow God's call.

ABOUT THE AUTHOR: Gordon T. Smith is president and professor of systematic and spiritual theology at Ambrose University College and Seminary in Calgary, Alberta. He is the author of many books, including *The Voice of Jesus: Discernment, Prayer and the Witness of the Spirit.*

◆ QUESTIONS

1. Smith suggests that our view of the work of God in the world is too narrow because we think of religious work as more sacred. How can we acknowledge the essential goodness and sacred potential of each occupation to which people may be called?

2. The author stresses that few things are so crucial to vocational integrity as self-knowledge (chap. 3). As you reflect on this, what in your opinion are the greatest obstacles to self-knowledge?

3. Smith states that in considering vocation it is essential to take into account a person's life stage (chap. 4). Think about those in your life at various stages. What can you do to encourage or empower them?

4. In chapter 5, the author highlights the importance of sabbath, implying that if we are faithful in our vocation it will be evident, at least in part, in our regular observance of sabbath. Do you agree? If not, why not?

5. Three great temptations—the lure of power, the inordinate desire for material security and the longing for prestige—can derail us from truly embracing our vocations (chap. 6). Is there one temptation to which you are most vulnerable, and what should you do to minimize its capacity to derail you vocationally?

6. The title of this book reflects the crucial question: Will we have the courage to do what we are being called to? What are the fears that keep people from doing what they are being called to do?

7. How can we help ourselves or others embrace new skills in order to fulfill a vocation?

8. Smith suggests that most, if not all, of us will fulfill our vocations in the company of others, as part of organizations (chap. 11). What role can you play to foster within your organization a capacity to encourage each person to thrive in their shared work toward a common mission?

9. A theme that comes up often in this book is thanksgiving, or gratitude. In your current life circumstances, for what are you thankful? In what ways are you experiencing the blessing of God?

CULTURE MAKING
Recovering Our Creative Calling

Andy Crouch

2009 *Christianity Today* Book Award winner!

Named one of *Publishers Weekly's* best books of 2008 (religion category).

The only way to change culture is to create culture, says Andy Crouch. For too long, Christians have had an insufficient view of culture and have waged misguided "culture wars." But we must reclaim the cultural mandate to be the creative cultivators that God designed us to be.

This landmark book is sure to be a rallying cry for a new generation of culturally creative Christians. Discover your calling and join the culture makers.

"I am hard-pressed to think of something that twenty-first-century American Christians need to read more."

Lauren F. Winner, assistant professor of Christian spirituality, Duke Divinity School, and author of *Girl Meets God*

"Culture Making is one of the few books taking the discussion about Christianity and culture to a new level. . . . I highly recommend it."

Tim Keller, pastor, Redeemer Presbyterian Church, author, *The Reason for God*

 ABOUT THE AUTHOR: Andy Crouch (M.Div., Boston University School of Theology) is executive editor of *Christianity Today*, where he was also executive producer of This Is Our City, a multiyear project featuring documentary video, reporting and essays about Christians seeking the flourishing of their cities.

INTERVARSITY PRESS

◆ QUESTIONS

1. "Culture is what we make of the world" (p. 23). What does this mean?

2. "There is no such thing as 'the Culture'" (p. 48). Do you agree or disagree? What implications does this have for how we talk about and interact with "culture"?

3. "The only way to change culture is to create more of it" (p. 67). What are examples of this in your own life or in society at large?

4. Christian contemporay music provides an example of Christians copying what was going on in popular culture. In what ways has this cultural strategy been problematic? In what ways has it been effective?

5. What is the significance of God's having Adam name the animals?

6. What does the transformation of the cross from a symbol of torture to a symbol of life suggest about the gospel's unique culture-making role?

7. The story of Babel is used often (chaps. 6, 7, 9, 10, 11, 14) to relate other Scripture passages and culture. How did this affect your understanding of culture in Scripture?

8. What, the author asks, will we spend our (eternal) time doing in the New Jerusalem? Does this differ from your own ideas of heaven?

9. Did you find yourself reading chapter 12 with impatience, relief or with something in between?

10. What are some of the dangers of reading God's intentions into historical events?

11. The author states that each of us can become saints like Mother Teresa. Does this thought seem realistic? Attractive?

12. The author describes "the 3, the 12 and the 120" as necessary in culture making. Who are your "3"?

13. What is the author's final exhortation for those who want to be culturally creative? Is it something you're excited to follow?

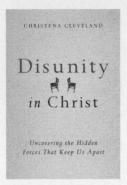

DISUNITY IN CHRIST

Uncovering the Hidden Forces That Keep Us Apart

Christena Cleveland

Despite Jesus' prayer that all Christians "be one," divisions have been epidemic in the body of Christ from the beginning to the present. We cluster in theological groups, gender groups, age groups, ethnic groups, educational and economic groups. We criticize freely those who disagree with us, don't look like us, don't act like us or don't like what we like.

Though we may think we know why this happens, Christena Cleveland says we probably don't.

With a personal touch and the trained eye of a social psychologist, Cleveland brings to bear the latest studies and research on the unseen dynamics at work that tend to separate us from others. Learn why Christians who have a heart for unity have such a hard time actually uniting.

Here are the tools we need to understand how we can overcome the hidden forces that divide us.

> *"Every Christian concerned about reconciliation in the church—and all Christians should be—will benefit from reading* Disunity in Christ.*"*
>
> **Greg Boyd, senior pastor, Woodland Hills Church, Maplewood, Minnesota**

ABOUT THE AUTHOR: Christena Cleveland (Ph.D., University of California, Santa Barbara) is a social psychologist who teaches at St. Catherine University in St. Paul, Minnesota. She consults with pastors and organizational leaders on multicultural issues and speaks regularly at conferences, schools and churches.

Connect with Christena at christenacleveland.com

INTERVARSITY PRESS

◆ QUESTIONS

1. What was your overall reaction to the book?

2. What ideas did you find most helpful?

3. Chapter one is "Right Christian, Wrong Christian." How would you tend to describe Right Christian and Wrong Christian from your own perspective?

4. Chapter 2 mentions advantages of diverse groups—like being more likely to come up with creative and effective ideas. What advantages have you seen in diverse groups?

5. Categorizing helps us, says Cleveland (pp. 46-48), because our brains can only deal with so much new information at one time. What are the downsides of categorizing?

6. Can you think of examples of when you've engaged in "we are unique; they are the same" thinking (pp. 51-54)?

7. How do you react to the idea of cognitive generosity, the ability to stop relying on inaccurate categories and see someone differently?

8. Has someone else ever held you to their cultural group's gold standard, suggesting that you or your group misses the mark by their measure (pp. 70-73)? How did you feel?

9. Think back to your earlier days as a junior high kid. Can you recall feeling the urge to BIRG (bask in reflected glory) or CORF (cut off reflected failure) in order to maintain self-esteem?

10. What do you think about the results of the Fein and Spencer study that looked at perceptions of Jewish versus non-Jewish women after people received positive or negative evaluations of themselves (pp. 106-7)?

11. Remember Randy the Hymn Lover in chapter 8. How has your own cultural background influenced your religious beliefs and practices?

12. In what ways are you a privileged/powerful person in your community?

13. What are some practical applications of this book for you?

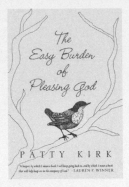

THE EASY BURDEN OF PLEASING GOD

Patty Kirk

Patty Kirk knows what it's like to try to impress God. It's like beating the air and bruising your soul.

In *The Easy Burden of Pleasing God* she reminds us, through stories and reflections and careful meditation on the Scriptures, that despite what we may have heard or told ourselves, the yoke we take on as we follow Jesus is easy, and the burden of a loving God is light. To all of us who pursue perfection in vain and ache with the defeat that follows, *The Easy Burden of Pleasing God* will be truly good news.

"I adore this little book. . . . Whether you are new in the life of faith, newly again in the life of faith or an old hand, Patty Kirk's wisdom—served up in prose that is the best kind of clear, and served up with humor and personality—will edify. In short, The Easy Burden of Pleasing God is a keeper, by which I mean a book I will keep going back to, and by which I mean a book that will help keep me in the company of God."

Lauren F. Winner, author of *Girl Meets God* and *Still: Notes on a Mid-Faith Crisis*

ABOUT THE AUTHOR: Patty Kirk is writer in residence and associate professor of English at John Brown University. She is an award-winning writer and author of *Confessions of an Amateur Believer* and *Starting from Scratch: Memoirs of a Wandering Cook.*

INTERVARSITY PRESS

◆ QUESTIONS

1. Read the final words of chapter 1. How do they make you feel?

2. Do you share the author's opinion that "our simultaneous desire and incapacity to do what God is offering to do for us is why many of us are unhappy in this life" (p. 35)?

3. Kirk stresses that some limitations actually promote freedom. What are some limitations on your life that are actually freeing and why?

4. What good things do you do out of obligation rather than enjoyment?

5. Does the explanation of "yoke" (pp. 90-91) help you hear Jesus' invitation "take my yoke upon you" differently?

6. Why is it so hard for us to say no? How can you better trust God to take care of what needs done, even if that means he uses someone else?

7. How might viewing the Bible as a rulebook affect your perception of love?

8. What areas of your faith have become burdens? Why?

9. How does chapter 22's explanation of Jesus' response to the rich young man help you understand Jesus' call to perfection in the Sermon on the Mount?

10. Are there any scriptural commands—literal or not—that you strive especially to follow? Have any of these become more of a priority in your life than God's work of believing in Jesus?

11. Kirk writes that she learned how to love God involuntarily and effortlessly when she reflected on people who loved her that way. Reflect on this love: how can you apply it to your relationship with God?

12. What is keeping you from surrendering to the kind of faith that Peter had when he stepped out of the boat?

EAT WITH JOY
Redeeming God's Gift of Food

Rachel Marie Stone
Foreword by Norman Wirzba

Our relationship with food is complicated to say the least.

Rachel Stone calls us to rediscover joyful eating by receiving food as God's good gift of provision and care for us. She shows us how God intends for us to relate to him and each other through food, and how our meals can become expressions of generosity, community and love of neighbor.

Filled with practical insights and some tasty recipes, this book provides a Christian journey into the delight of eating. Come to the table, partake of the Bread of Life—and eat with joy.

> *"Rachel Marie Stone is a woman after my own heart: a mom, a writer and a Christian who loves to feed the people she cares about. Eat with Joy is practical and inspiring, wise and full of love."*
>
> **Shauna Niequist, author of *Cold Tangerines* and *Bittersweet*, www.shaunaniequist.com**

ABOUT THE AUTHOR: Rachel Marie Stone is a regular writer for Christianity Today's *Her.meneutics* blog. She has also written for such publications as *Christianity Today, Books & Culture, Catapult, Relevant, Flourish* and *The Huffington Post*. She enjoys gardening and meal-making with her husband and two sons.

She is coeditor (with Timothy Stone and Julius Steinberg) of the forthcoming book *The Shape of the Writings*.

Connect with Rachel at rachelmariestone.com

INTERVARSITY PRESS

◆ QUESTIONS

1. The author says that "God made eating sustaining, delicious and pleasurable because God is all those things and more" (p. 24). How do you respond to this statement?

2. What assumptions do you have regarding the eating habits of people who are poor? Were they challenged by this chapter?

3. What goes through your mind when you read something like "Even people who have never heard the name of Jesus know the name of Coke" (p. 52)?

4. "Food and its preparation are the foundations of families and even of cultures" (p. 67). Do you agree? What does our foundation look like today?

5. Have you experienced the decline of the family meal in your lifetime? What do you think causes the decline and what are its effects?

6. How might eating be more restorative and healing in the lives of those around you?

7. What changes in your diet are you considering after reading chapter 5 on sustainable eating?

8. How is food culture related to culture making more broadly?

9. What does Robert Farrar Capon mean when he says calories are "idols" (p. 138)?

10. Does inexpensive and readily available prepared food discourage you from cooking?

11. In chapter 7 the author describes how people often assume she's about to judge their dietary habits. Have you experienced dietary judgmentalism? What forms does it take?

12. The author writes, "Choosing the 'right' kind of food (whatever that is) is much less important to me than giving thanks to God and being kind to my neighbor." How is that different from or similar to your own perspective?

13. Did you try any recipes from the book? Which were your favorites?

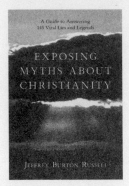

EXPOSING MYTHS ABOUT CHRISTIANITY
A Guide to Answering 145 Viral Lies and Legends

Jeffrey Burton Russell

Renowned historian Jeffrey Burton Russell turns to the serious questions that confront Christianity in contemporary culture. He examines a wide array of common misperceptions, characterizations, stereotypes, caricatures and outright myths about Christianity that circulate heavily within today's society and are even believed by many Christians. In succinct and engaging manner, Russell sets the record straight against the New Atheists and other cultural critics who charge Christianity with being outdated, destructive, superstitious, unenlightened, racist, colonialist, based on fabrication and other significant false accusations.

> *"This is Christian apologetics at its best.... What C. S. Lewis's* Mere Christianity *did in the 1940s, Jeffrey Burton Russell has done for us. For those seeking and for those who doubt, this is a must-read book."*
>
> **Very Rev. Dr. Ian Markham, president and professor of theology, Virginia Theological Seminary**

ABOUT THE AUTHOR: Jeffrey Burton Russell (Ph.D., Emory University) was a history professor at the University of California, Santa Barbara from 1979 to 1998 where he is now a professor of history, emeritus. Russell has published numerous books and articles on his area of expertise, the history of theology. Early in his academic career, Russell was honored as a Fulbright Fellow, Harvard Junior Fellow and Guggenheim Fellow.

INTERVARSITY PRESS

◆ QUESTIONS

1. The author says that, because of widespread myths, lies and legends among Christians and non-Christians alike, "it has become difficult to discuss Christianity openly, knowledgeably and fairly" (p. 17). In what ways have you experienced this difficulty in your own life and relationships?

2. The author rejects the claim that "religion causes more war and suffering than atheism" (pp. 55-58). Do you think he has made a strong case? Explain.

3. Christianity has been labeled as "stupid" for a variety of reasons (pp. 131-182). Have you or someone you know experienced ridicule or condescension in response to expressing Christian convictions?

4. The author says that "science and Christianity examine evidence in different ways. Their methods are different, but their findings or results are compatible" (p. 147). Does your culture tend to see Christianity and science as compatible or as antagonistic? Give examples.

5. One belief the author addresses is that there were originally many versions of Christianity, which were suppressed in favor of one official version (pp. 208-11). How does the author debunk this myth?

6. Jesus' death on the cross for our sins can sound like Christian's believe that God had his own Son "tortured and murdered." How does the author expose this as a "misunderstanding of the relationship of Jesus to God in Christian teaching" (p. 241)?

7. Many scientists and philosophers assume that "miracles are impossible" (pp. 301-10). What are some ways common assumptions about what is possible or impossible might affect how we look at testimony claiming to support miraculous occurrences?

8. The author claims that "Christians are much less interested in 'religion' than they are in Jesus" (p. 326). Explain why you agree or disagree with this statement.

9. In response to the idea that "nothing is true" (pp. 335-39), the author claims that truth is ultimately grounded in the God who is Truth, so that "truth is not dry and bloodless" (p. 338). What does it mean to live as a person who seeks truth (and Truth)?

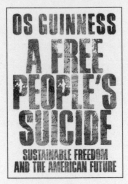

A FREE PEOPLE'S SUICIDE

Sustainable Freedom and the American Future

Os Guinness

2013 *Logos* Book of the Year in Christianity/Culture!

Cultural observer Os Guinness argues that the American experiment in freedom is at risk. Summoning historical evidence on how democracies evolve, Guinness shows that contemporary views of freedom are unsustainable because they undermine the conditions necessary for freedom to thrive. He calls us to reconsider the audacity of sustainable freedom and what it would take to restore it.

The future of the republic depends on whether Americans will rise to the challenge of living up to America's unfulfilled potential for freedom, both for itself and for the world.

"Sometimes a book is so important and so timely that not to have read it is to embarrass oneself. This is such a book. Its message is so crucial and so clear that all Americans are obligated to read it and have a national conversation on its themes. No cultural commentator or politician who has not read this book should ever be taken seriously again. Let this book be the new litmus test."

Eric Metaxas, author of *Bonhoeffer: Pastor, Martyr, Prophet, Spy* and *Amazing Grace: William Wilberforce and the Heroic Campaign to End Slavery*

ABOUT THE AUTHOR: Os Guinness (D.Phil., Oxford) is the author or editor of more than twenty-five books, including *Time for Truth* and *The Case for Civility*. A frequent speaker and prominent social critic, he is founder of the Trinity Forum and has been a visiting fellow at the Brookings Institution and a guest scholar at the Woodrow Wilson Center for International Studies.

View a video of Os at ivpress.com/guinnessvideos.

INTERVARSITY PRESS

◆ QUESTIONS

1. What motivated you to read this book? What concerns you about how freedom is lived out or expressed today?

2. What does the book's title mean? What is the author's main concern for how Americans think about their freedom?

3. What is the difference between negative freedom and positive freedom? When people or media talk about "our freedom," in what ways do they mean it?

4. How might unfettered freedom become unhealthy or self-defeating? What might be some dangers of an overemphasis on unrestricted, irresponsible freedom?

5. How is true freedom different from mere consumer choices and options?

6. What is the difference between winning freedom, ordering freedom and sustaining freedom?

7. What does the author mean by "sustainable freedom"? In what ways might freedom be made more sustainable?

8. What does the author mean by the "golden triangle of freedom" (chap. 4)? How do these three elements relate to each other?

9. The author describes the Jewish and Christian perspective of freedom as a gift, as a relationship and as truth (chap. 5). What is the significance of each of these? What might be some implications for how we understand and live out our freedom?

10. What lessons might America learn from the experience of previous empires?

11. What practical solutions are needed to address the challenges of sustainable freedom? What needs to happen at local levels? At national and societal levels?

12. After reading this book, are you more or less hopeful about the prospects for freedom in American society and around the world? How might you approach life differently in light of what you have read and discussed?

THE GIRL IN THE ORANGE DRESS

Searching for a Father Who Does Not Fail

Margot Starbuck

When Margot Starbuck's adoptive parents divorced, her dad moved east, and her mom and dad each got remarried, she told herself that she was extra loved since she had more than two parents and people in different times zones who cared about her.

But the word she really believed about herself was *rejected*. First by her birthparents. Then by her adoptive father when he moved away. Then by her stepfather. Then by her birthfather a second time when she tried to invite him into her life.

Most of all, Margot felt rejected by God, whom she also suspected could not be trusted. Margot's story begins with a woman looking for her biological father. But it doesn't end when she finds him. Instead, his rejection punctures her soul and sends her on a different search—one that leads to a different Father whose love can never fail.

> *"I haven't felt this much emotion from a memoir since reading* Angela's Ashes. *. . . Humbly honest, graciously hilarious, evocative."*
>
> **Lisa Samson, author of *Quaker Summer, Justice in the Burbs* and *The Church Ladies***

ABOUT THE AUTHOR: Margot Starbuck is an author and speaker equipping Christians to live love. She speaks around the country and is the author of four books, including *Small Things with Great Love*.

INTERVARSITY PRESS

◆ QUESTIONS

1. In the first chapter, Margot describes the way she navigated a rocky home life by smiling and pretending everything was fine. What are other ways a child might attempt to manage the unavoidable bumps of childhood?

2. During college, Margot became convinced that God loved others, but she was less able to embrace God's love for her (p. 49). In your experience, has it been easier to believe that God loved others or that God loved you? Why?

3. Can you point to particular events in your own life—or the life of someone you know—which have dismantled reliable defenses?

4. Margot continued desperately to search for love in the face of her birthfather, Max, in chapter 4. In what ways do human faces and relationships satisfy our deep needs? How do they fail?

5. Margot finally embraced the journey toward healing when the pain of not doing so became unbearable. Do you take intentional steps to face your own life's losses or do you engage with conflict only when circumstances have forced you to?

6. Rather than trying to "protect" God any longer, in chapter 9 Margot finally raises her fist and gets angry. Have you ever reached the point where you were willing to engage in healthy conflict with another person or with God? How did it turn out?

7. With the ears of her heart, Margot heard God's voice speaking the words, "I am for you." Were you to tip your face toward God's, how easy or difficult would it be for you to receive these words? Do they ring true in your experience or fall flat?

8. In the closing paragraphs of the book, as Margot imagines God writing her name on his palm, she knows that name which God uses for her to be "beloved." What would be the affectionate name God would use for you?

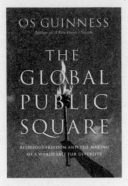

THE GLOBAL PUBLIC SQUARE

Religious Freedom and the Making of a World Safe for Diversity

Os Guinness

In a world torn by religious conflict, the threats to human dignity are terrifyingly real. How do we live with our deepest differences?

Os Guinness argues that the way forward for the world lies in promoting freedom of religion and belief for people of all faiths and none. He sets out a vision of a civil and cosmopolitan global public square, and how it can be established by championing the freedom of the soul—the inviolable freedom of thought, conscience and religion.

Far from utopian, this constructive vision charts a course for the future of the world. For a world desperate for hope at a critical juncture of human history, here is a way forward, for the good of all.

> *"This is a book that should be read by everyone concerned with freedom of conscience."*
>
> **Peter L. Berger, professor emeritus, Boston University**

ABOUT THE AUTHOR: Os Guinness (D.Phil., Oxford) is the author or editor of more than twenty-five books, including *Time for Truth* and *The Case for Civility*. A frequent speaker and prominent social critic, he is founder of the Trinity Forum and has been a visiting fellow at the Brookings Institution and a guest scholar at the Woodrow Wilson Center for International Studies.

INTERVARSITY PRESS

◆ QUESTIONS

1. The author has written this book to help humankind live at peace with one another even in the midst of deep differences. In what ways do you see local or global conflicts arise out of such differences? What are the dangers to society if such conflicts are not resolved?

2. What does the author mean by "soul freedom"? How is soul freedom good for people of all faiths or none?

3. What is the relationship between civil society and freedom of thought, conscience and religion?

4. How is religious freedom threatened today? Where have you seen or experienced contemporary challenges to soul freedom?

5. How might religious freedom contribute fruitfully to public life?

6. In what ways do conservatives sometimes act unconservatively? In what ways do liberals sometimes act illiberally? How does the author correct these approaches?

7. What does the author mean by the "making of a world safe for diversity"?

8. What are the dangers of a "naked public square" that restricts religious belief?

9. What are the dangers of a "sacred public square" that promotes a particular kind of religious belief?

10. What are the advantages of a "civil public square"? What might this look like in our society today?

11. In what ways might responsible religious and secularist leaders work together for the common good of humankind? What examples do you look to for such partnership?

12. Review the text of the Global Charter of Conscience. What strikes you most about this document? How does it inform your perspective on current events and global affairs?

13. After reading this book, are you encouraged or discouraged about the prospects for a more peaceful, civil world? What are your hopes for the future of society and the global common good?

GOD BEHAVING BADLY

Is the God of the Old Testament Angry, Sexist and Racist?

David T. Lamb

God has a bad reputation. Many think of God as wrathful and angry, smiting people right and left for no apparent reason. The Old Testament in particular seems at times to portray God as capricious and malevolent, wiping out armies and nations, punishing enemies with extreme prejudice.

But the story is more complicated than that. Alongside troubling passages of God's punishment and judgment are pictures of God's love, forgiveness and slowness to anger. Can God be trusted or not?

David Lamb unpacks the complexity of the Old Testament to explore God's character. He provides historical and cultural background to shed light on problematic passages and to bring underlying themes to the fore. Without minimizing the sometimes harsh realities of the biblical record, Lamb assembles an overall portrait that gives coherence to our understanding of God in both the Old and New Testaments.

"I will require my college students to read this book. I became sensitive to the 'God questions' in the Bible because students asked me questions that came straight from troubled hearts."

Scot McKnight, Northern Seminary

ABOUT THE AUTHOR: David T. Lamb (D.Phil., Oxford) is associate professor of Old Testament at Biblical Theological Seminary in Hatfield, Pennsylvania. He previously worked in campus ministry with InterVarsity Christian Fellowship and has taught extensively in various crosscultural contexts.

INTERVARSITY PRESS

◆ QUESTIONS

1. What negative images of the God of the Old Testament do you or people you know have?

2. Which Old Testament passages do you find problematic, confusing or bizarre?

3. Have you ever worried that God would punish you or strike you down for something you did? What was it?

4. When is it good to be angry? How does a person find the right balance between appropriate anger and steadfast love in relationships?

5. Which curse is worse—the man's or the woman's (Genesis 3:16-19)? Why do you think so?

6. Why do you think Jesus praised the woman who anointed his feet so dramatically?

7. What makes the story of the hospitable Samaritan such a popular story?

8. How can you be more like Saint Francis in befriending people of different races or different faiths?

9. Why did the biblical authors include so much violence and warfare? Should they have edited some of that out?

10. How can you promote peace and reconciliation in your family, school, job and neighborhood?

11. Which Old or New Testament law does not make sense to you? Why do you think God would command it?

12. Do you ever feel like Jonah and wish that God wasn't merciful to someone? What types of people make you feel this way? Why?

13. How comfortable do you feel complaining or lamenting to God?

14. What is the percentage of mobsters and prostitutes in your church? How can you increase that percentage to make your community more like Jesus'?

15. What is your favorite word to describe God? Why? How can you become more like God in this respect?

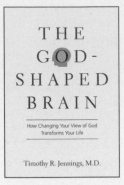

THE GOD-SHAPED BRAIN

How Changing Your View of God Transforms Your Life

Timothy R. Jennings, M.D.

Brain research has found that our thoughts and beliefs affect our physical, mental and spiritual health. When we understand God as good and loving, we flourish. Unfortunately, many of us have distorted images of God and mostly think of him in fearful, punitive ways. This leads us into unhealthy patterns of self-defeating behaviors and toxic relationships.

Psychiatrist Tim Jennings unveils how our brains and bodies thrive when we have a healthy understanding of who God is. He dispels common misconceptions about God and shows how different God concepts affect the brain differently. Our brains can adapt, change and rewire with redeemed thinking that frees us from unnecessary pain and suffering. Discover how science and Scripture come together to bring healing and transformation to our lives.

> *"Read this book to know God more fully. Read this book to know your brain more fully. And see how knowing God will change your brain—and your life—in ways you never thought possible."*
>
> **Curt Thompson, M.D., psychiatrist and author of *Anatomy of the Soul***

ABOUT THE AUTHOR: Timothy R. Jennings, M.D., is a board certified Christian psychiatrist, speaker and author. He is a fellow of the American Psychiatric Association and president-elect of the Tennessee Psychiatric Association. He also serves on the board of the Southern Psychiatric Association and is in private practice in Tennessee.

INTERVARSITY PRESS

◆ QUESTIONS

1. Consider some of the fundamental beliefs you have about God and life. How do you think these beliefs were formed and how are they influenced by the social environment surrounding you?

2. What examples in science and nature can you think of that demonstrate the idea illustrated in chapter 1 about the law of love as a circular process of giving and receiving?

3. How do Jennings's explanations about the interworking of the brain help you to understand the imbalance or conflict occurring between fear and love in our heads?

4. Jennings states on page 70 that he "needed the living Word to define the Written word." How can Jesus reframe the way you understand not just the Bible but also God?

5. Section II includes many examples from Jennings's counseling experience to demonstrate the lies people believe about God and how that conflict breaks the circle of love and trust. Which story did you relate to most and why?

6. In chapter 12, Jennings suggests a unique understanding of God's record books and the forgiving of sins by using the analogy of a doctor and medical records. How does this explanation hold up, or not, with what you believe about God?

7. What does Jennings suggest as the critical difference between Jesus and Buddha, as well as between God's law of love and the systems of imposed law or Eastern philosophy?

8. In prefacing the book, Jennings writes, "Although we have power over what we believe, what we believe holds real power over us—power to heal and power to destroy" (p. 9). He revisits this statement on page 219 posing this final question: What do you believe about God?

HOLY IS THE DAY
Living in the Gift of the Present

Carolyn Weber

holy is the day
Living in the Gift of the Present

CAROLYN WEBER
author of Surprised by Oxford

We know rest and reflection are necessary for a healthy life—even Jesus took time to get away from the crowds, away from the demands of everyday life, to pray, to spend time with close friends, to sleep.

But when Carolyn Weber—emotionally and physically exhausted from managing her career as a college professor, writing her first book and parenting three children under the age of three—hears this truth from a friend, all she can think is: but who will do everything if I don't?

And this sets her on a journey to find the still, small space in each day.

In these pages Carolyn reflects on the eternal beauty that lurks within the present. Drawing from literature, history and everyday life, *Holy Is the Day* is a collection of spiritual reflections and poignant stories that trace the way God's ever-renewing grace is a gift of the present.

> *"Carolyn Weber lives gracefully and writes elegantly. Her poetic eyes search beneath the surface. . . . This is a beautiful book that spoke to my heart and changed my day."*
>
> **Randy Alcorn, author of *If God Is Good* and *Deception***

ABOUT THE AUTHOR: Carolyn Weber (D. Phil., University of Oxford) is an author, speaker and teacher who has specialized in eighteenth- and nineteenth-century British and European literature. She has recently taught English literature at Seattle Pacific University and Westmont College. She is the author of *Surprised by Oxford: A Memoir.*

Listen to an interview with Carolyn at ivpress.com/holy-is-the-day.

INTERVARSITY PRESS

◆ QUESTIONS

1. How does the birth story in the opening chapter prepare us for themes to be explored in the book?

2. On page 39, the author quotes a line from a T. S. Eliot play: "You don't need therapy, you need salvation." The author concedes to needing both. What are your cultural and/or personal thoughts on these two poles?

3. How has your life been affected by what the author terms a "U-turn friend"?

4. How does practicing *carpe Deum* challenge your spiritual walk?

5. "Trauma prepares us for resurrection," claims the author. Have you found this to be the case in your own life?

6. The author identifies Scripture, prayer and fellowship as forms of "manna," or ways that we are fed God's provision in proportion from his hand. Which of these ways do you find most fulfilling or, conversely, troubling?

7. How do you understand the act of "holy waiting" as discussed in chapter 11?

8. Discuss the following statement: "It is the loving, not the longing, that matters most" (p. 148).

9. Think of the author's description of time in the first chapter (p. 33) or the distinction between *chronos* and *kairos* in the final chapter (p. 184). How does the author illustrate notions of time?

10. Even Jesus went out in a boat, as this book reminds us. How does this inform your understanding of God as man and particularly his relationship to us?

11. What are some practical ways to practice retreat with our Lord in our day-to-day, busy lives?

12. At the very end of the book, the author notes how the Hebrew word *Hosanna* stands for both "help" and "praise." She identifies it as the shortest psalm, the single-worded prayer that says it all. Do you see these entities (help and praise) as separate or interrelated?

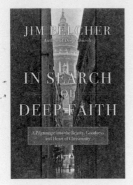

IN SEARCH OF DEEP FAITH

A Pilgrimage into the Beauty, Goodness and Heart of Christianity

Jim Belcher

In the post-Christian world, many have given up on faith of any kind, finding it shallow and unsatisfying. Why bother with Christianity?

After a draining season of life, pastor Jim Belcher and his family spent a year traveling through Europe, seeking answers for these questions and exploring the faith that has shaped civilizations throughout the centuries. Through the experiences of William Wilberforce, Vincent van Gogh, Corrie ten Boom and others, Belcher saw glimpses of insight, beauty and courage that transcended human limitations. He found himself surprised by joy and compelled by faith.

Whether you are giving up on Christianity or encountering it for the first time, you are invited to come along on this pilgrimage.

> *"The first chapter was my favorite—until I read the second. . . . Chapter by chapter, Jim takes you and your family on a practical theology pilgrimage through Europe that will expand your vision for Christ-centered living. You'll be thinking about it and talking about it long after you finish the final page."*
>
> **Kara Powell, executive director, Fuller Youth Institute, Fuller Theological Seminary**

ABOUT THE AUTHOR: Jim Belcher (Ph.D., Georgetown) is associate professor of practical theology at Knox Theological Seminary. He is the founding and former lead pastor of Redeemer Presbyterian Church (PCA) in Newport Beach, California. He is the author of *Deep Church*.

View a video of Jim on Bonhoeffer at ivpress.com/deepfaith.

◆ QUESTIONS

1. The author embarked on a pilgrimage with his family to find, among other things, "rest for my soul" (p. 13). What would your reason be for taking a pilgrimage?

2. The author talks about losing desire (p. 44). Why do you think the story of Van and Davy helped him get it back?

3. The author writes, "Lewis believed fairy tales begin to work on our hearts and minds, calling us to grander things; they stir a longing for heaven, our true home" (p. 103). Do you agree? Why or why not?

4. The author concludes in chapter 5, "For a person with a calling, education plays an important role" (p. 131). Why do you think education is vital to a person's calling?

5. "Beauty rightly understood—broken beauty . . . has the ability . . . to steer us between twin dangers: decadence and sentimentalism" (p. 167) but it also has the ability to steer us to true beauty. What would you describe as broken beauty, and how do you think it can guide us?

6. Do you agree with the statement "The reason most young people adopt a kind of moral relativism is because they are petrified of any type of fundamentalism and extremism. " (p. 175) Why or why not?

7. Chapter 7 relates the story of Corrie ten Boom. Despite her suffering she did not despair. What did her story teach you about suffering?

8. The author says Bonhoeffer had an eschatological imagination. He did not just think about hope he lived it. How does this understanding help you in your search for deep faith?

9. In Heidelberg, the author discovered that if his family was to be "wholeheartedly willing and ready from now on to live for him [God]," they had to learn from all the heroes they had studied and experienced (P. 281).) What have you learned in following the author and his family on this pilgrimage?

THE ISRAELI-PALESTINIAN CONFLICT

Tough Questions, Direct Answers
The Skeptic's Guide™ Series

Dale Hanson Bourke

With all of the heat surrounding the Israeli-Palestinian conflict, even the most basic facts can be hard to grasp.

In this Skeptic's Guide™, Dale Hanson Bourke sheds light on the places, terms, history and current issues shaping this important region. Offering an even-handed presentation of a range of views on the most controversial issues, she answers such tough questions as:

- What is meant by a two-state solution?
- Who are the Palestinian Christians?
- How does the Arab Spring affect the conflict?

Easy to read and understand, this dynamic guide offers the type of presentation that has made the Skeptic's Guide™ series so popular with individuals and groups.

> *"Slowly, inexorably and beautifully, Dale Hanson Bourke untangles the jumbled mess and separates fact from fiction. What's even more beautiful is that she leaves the conclusions to you—a rare gift indeed."*
>
> **Nancy Ortberg, author of *Looking for God***

ABOUT THE AUTHOR: Dale Hanson Bourke is president of PDI, a marketing and communications strategy firm. The author of ten books, she often speaks and writes on international development and women's issues. Previously SVP at World Relief, Bourke has also served as publisher of Religion News Service and editor of *Today's Christian Woman,* and was a nationally syndicated columnist.

INTERVARSITY PRESS

◆ QUESTIONS

1. "In those earliest days of spiritual education and Sunday school stories," the author writes, "I somehow confused the Holy Land with heaven" (p. 9). Does this region have any special quality as you imagine it? Explain.

2. Why do you think the Israeli-Palestinian conflict raises such strong feelings for people?

3. Why (or why not) should Christians in the United States be concerned about the Israeli-Palestinian conflict?

4. What in this book surprised you about the modern history of the Palestinians?

5. What surprised you about the role of the United States in the region?

6. What surprised you about the ancient history of the region?

7. Think of one issue in the contemporary conflict that is particularly compelling to you. How do you think the various parties in the conflict could contribute to resolving that issue?

8. Many of the most urgent problems in the Middle East are not political but existential: poverty, violence and so on. At a practical level, what can people in the West do to alleviate suffering in the Middle East?

9. The Israeli-Palestinian conflict is often complicated by the heated rhetoric surrounding the issues. What rules would you propose for debating different convictions about the conflict?

10. "As I researched and wrote this book," the author reports, "the two questions I was asked most often were, 'Is there hope to end the conflict?' and 'Have you decided who is wrong and who is right?'" (p. 132). Before you read this book, who had you decided was wrong or right? Has that impression changed? Explain.

11. Before you read this book, did you have hope for an end to the Israeli-Palestinian conflict? Has that changed? Explain.

12. "People of faith need to pray, not for one side or the other but that God would move in unexpected ways to bring peace to the land and the people in a way that is truly holy" (p. 132). What, in your mind, does "peace . . . that is truly holy" look like?

Excerpt from . . . *Israeli-Palestinian Conflict*

For Christians, Abraham's descendants are traced through ancient Israel's King David to Jesus. The apostle Paul preached in the New Testament that those who believe in Jesus become part of the spiritual lineage. "Understand, then, that those who have faith are children of Abraham" (Gal 3:7).

Were Arabs and Jews always at war?

"It has in fact been less than a century since Jews and Arabs began to view one another as enemies."

Mark Tessler

Historians say that Arabs and Jews lived together both peacefully and with common purposes for centuries. Mark Tessler, in his extensive history of the Israeli-Palestinian conflict, says that "it has in fact been less than a century since Jews and Arabs began to view one another as enemies."[1]

Throughout history, Arabs and Jews often had a common enemy. The Crusades, for example, resulted in the slaughter of Muslims and Jews, as well as the indigenous Arab Christian populations who were considered pagan.

Father Elias Chacour, a Christian Palestinian who grew up in the village of Biram, writes in his book *Blood Brothers* about his childhood experience living at peace with his Jewish neighbors. He makes the case for peace based on a shared heritage: "We had suffered together under the Romans, Persians, Crusaders and Turks, and learned to share the simple elements of human existence—faith, reverence for life, hospitality."[2] In recent history, Israel has negotiated peace treaties with Arab countries. Egypt and Jordan have long-standing peace agreements with Israel.

Why is Jerusalem
so important in history?

Jerusalem is often translated as "peace" or "city of peace," but the city has been in the middle of conflict for much of the last four thousand years. According to the book *Jerusalem Besieged*, the city has been destroyed twice, besieged twenty-three times, attacked fifty-two times, and captured and recaptured forty-four times.[3]

Jerusalem is important in Judaism because David captured the city and first ruled from it as king over all the tribes of Israel. The first Jewish temple was built there by King Solomon; it was later destroyed by the Babylonians. The second temple was built after the fall of the Babylonians; eventually it was desecrated by the Hellenists, rededicated and later destroyed by the Romans. Some religious Jews believe that a third temple will be rebuilt in Jerusalem after the Messiah comes. Some Christians believe it will be rebuilt when Jesus returns.

Hadrian ruled Jerusalem in the second century, renamed and paganized it, and banned Jews from the city. The Emperor Constantine reclaimed the city as Christian in the fourth century, built the Church of the Holy Sepulcher and made it a center of Christian pilgrimage. (The Greek Orthodox Church traces its roots to this period.) Important to Christians as the city where Jesus was crucified, resurrected and ascended to heaven, it is also where the Pentecost event in Acts 2 occurred.

By the seventh century the city had come under Muslim rule, and the Dome of the Rock was built over the rock from which Muhammad is said to have as-

> "My peaceful homeland of Palestine, known as the Holy Land, had become a land of war."
>
> Fr. Elias Chacour

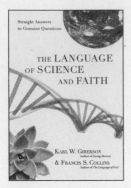

THE LANGUAGE OF SCIENCE AND FAITH

Straight Answers to Genuine Questions

Karl W. Giberson and Francis S. Collins

World-renowned scientists Francis Collins, author of *The Language of God,* and Karl Giberson show how we can embrace both science and biblical faith.

Together they clearly answer dozens of the most common questions people ask about Darwin, evolution, the age of the earth, the Bible, the existence of God and our finely tuned universe. They also consider how their views stack up against the new atheists as well as against creationists and adherents of intelligent design.

Disentangling falsehoods from contemporary research, they uncover a story of a beautiful world made by a supremely creative God.

"This book is at the top of my recommendations both as an evaluation of theories of creation and as a devotional that prompts us to revere the Creator."

Joel C. Hunter, Northland Church, Longwood, Florida

ABOUT THE AUTHORS: Karl W. Giberson (Ph.D.) is an internationally known scholar, speaker and writer. He directs the Science & Religion writing workshop at Gordon College. Giberson has written nine books, including *Saving Darwin.* He lives on the web at www.karlgiberson.com.

Francis S. Collins (M.D., Ph.D.) is a world-renowned physician-geneticist known for spearheading the Human Genome Project, which produced the first complete sequence of human DNA. He has served as the director of the National Institutes of Health since 2009. He is the author of *The Language of God,* which spent fourteen weeks on the *New York Times* bestseller list.

INTERVARSITY PRESS

◆ QUESTIONS

1. Describe your experience regarding the intersection of questions of science and faith—in your personal life, through your education, or through your church or religious context.

2. The authors make a distinction between evolution "in the most general sense" being characterized as "change over time" and evolution in the "biological" sense being "the way that species from the past developed into the diverse roster of species that exist today" (p. 34). Why is gaining an understanding of these two distinct uses of the word important to a fruitful discussion of the topic?

3. In chapter 3 of *The Language of Science and Faith*, the authors ask, "Do science and religion have to overlap?" How would you answer their question?

4. The authors say that "science and religion answer different questions or answer the same question in different ways," and they utilize an analogy attributed to Cambridge University physicist John Polkinghorne regarding the question "Why is the water in the tea kettle boiling?" (p. 107). In what ways did their use of that analogy illuminate their point for you?

5. The authors suggest that Charles Darwin had defenders and that it's a misconception that Christians greeted his theory with immediate hostility. Why might Darwin be more controversial with some Christians today than he was in his own time? Ch6 p152

6. In chapter 8, the authors offer three theological speculations concerning God's role in evolution. How do you respond to their assertions?

7. How do different interpretations of the beginning of the book of Genesis—including the account of Adam and Eve—change the significance of that portion of the Bible in your own life?

8. Beginning on page 216, the authors convey what they call the "modern creation story." How do you respond to this account of creation?

9. In what ways did your reading of *The Language of Science and Faith* clarify the subject matter for you?

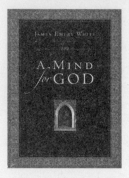

A MIND FOR GOD

James Emery White

To be fully human is to *think*.

The apostle Paul calls us to "take captive every thought to make it obedient to Christ" (2 Corinthians 10:5). But James Emery White fears that Western Christians are failing in this task. Because we have not developed good intellectual habits, our minds instead have been captured by our culture.

A Mind for God is written to help us break free from this cultural captivity through the spiritual and intellectual disciplines of reading, study and reflection. This inspirational and practical "rule for the mind" encourages and enables us to develop our minds for God.

Includes book lists and resources so you can "grow your brain."

"God wants us to have the mind of Christ. But what is that mind and how do we get it? James Emery White answers these questions in some of the most lucid prose being written today. A pleasure to read! A joy to take his advice!"

James W. Sire, author of *The Universe Next Door* **and** *Learning to Pray Through the Psalms*

ABOUT THE AUTHOR: James Emery White is the founding and senior pastor of Mecklenburg Community Church in Charlotte, North Carolina.

White is the author of over a dozen books, including such Gold Medallion nominees as *Serious Times* and *A Search for the Spiritual, Christianity Today* Book of the Year award-winner *Wrestling with God,* as well as *The Prayer God Longs For.*

For White's blog and further resources visit churchandulture.org.

◆ QUESTIONS

1. What does it mean, according to this book, to have a Christian mind?

2. In chapter 2, White asks provocatively, "Do Christians have anything to offer the world that it does not already have?" What is the importance of the mind in shaping the answers to his question?

3. White explains, "The understanding inherent within education is that there are certain facts that should be known, books that should be read, lives that should be studied, events that should be remembered and ideas that should be understood." Why should these these things be remembered, understood or read?

4. The author challenges us, as he does his students, by saying, "The Bible gives us all we must know, but not all that there is to know." What does this mean for the importance of things like reflection and thinking?

5. White points out, "A rule for learning is a matter of choice. The opportunities themselves are endless." What choices can you make in your life to create rules for learning?

6. How does developing a mind for God tie in to the Great Commission?

7. White suggests that the reason C. S. Lewis is held in such high regard is his mind. "Lewis is a hero because he was a Christian intellect who stepped forward to engage the world." How can you step forward and engage the world with your own intellect?

8. "As a monk in Normandy wrote in 1170: 'A monastery without a library [*sine armario*] is like a castle without an armory [*sine armamentario*]. Our library is our armory.'" Why would the monk understand a library as serving the same purpose as an armory?

9. What would the author say is involved in Christian reflection?

10. In the introduction White quotes Winston Churchill in an address to Harvard University in 1943 as saying, "The empires of the future will be empires of the mind." If that is true, what significance does it hold for the development of the Christian mind?

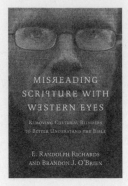

MISREADING SCRIPTURE WITH WESTERN EYES

Removing Cultural Blinders to Better Understand the Bible

E. Randolph Richards
and Brandon J. O'Brien

What was clear to the original readers of Scripture is not always clear to us. Because of the cultural distance between the biblical world and our contemporary setting, we often bring modern Western biases to the text.

Biblical scholars Brandon O'Brien and Randy Richards identify nine key areas where modern Westerners often misunderstand the cultural dynamics of the Bible. Drawing on their own crosscultural experience in global mission, O'Brien and Richards show how better self-awareness and understanding of cultural differences in language, time and social mores allow us to see the Bible in fresh and unexpected ways.

> *"The reader will leave the book with plenty of challenging questions to ask about approaches to Scripture. Interesting, thoughtful, and user-friendly."*
>
> **Philip Jenkins, author of *The Next Christendom***

ABOUT THE AUTHORS: E. Randolph Richards is dean of the School of Ministry and professor of biblical studies at Palm Beach Atlantic University in West Palm Beach, Florida.

Brandon J. O'Brien is a part-time instructor of religion at the College of DuPage and editor-at-large for *Leadership* journal with Christianity Today. O'Brien is author of *The Strategically Small Church*.

 INTERVARSITY PRESS

◆ QUESTIONS

1. The authors want this book to enrich your reading of the Bible, yet learning to read a text differently can be unsettling. What risks do you see in opening yourself up to new readings?

2. Mores are often generational. How do you think differently about specific cultural mores (such as drinking alcohol, dancing or sexual behavior) than your parents or grandparents? What role does culture play in the way these three generations view mores?

3. Imagine retelling the story of Ruth and Boaz today and saying, "Boaz the Israeli" and "Ruth the Palestinian." How might that affect how you read the story?

4. The authors give three assumptions regarding the way we view language: sufficiency, equivalency and clarity. Which assumption affects your reading of Scripture most?

5. In chapter 4 the differences between individualistic and collectivistic are explained. What are the dangers of reading the Bible through a collectivistic lens rather than an individualistic one? What is at stake for you?

6. What in chapter 5 on honor and shame was most surprising to you? Did it make you look at any particular Scripture verse differently?

7. "Sometimes translated 'season,' *kairos* time is when something important happens at just the right time" (p. 142). How does the fact that we typically think in *chronos* time (exact time) affect our understanding of Scripture?

8. The authors tell a story (p. 161-2) of a household helper, Sonya, in Indonesia. The author and Sonya had quite different expectations of this arrangement. What was your reaction to his story?

9. The authors claim that Americans are becoming more self-centerd (p. 194). How does this cause us to misread the Bible?

10. From the list, which pieces of advice will you follow: embrace complexity, beware of overcorrection, be teachable, embrace error, read together?

PLAYING GOD
Redeeming the Gift of Power

Andy Crouch

Power corrupts—as we've seen time and time again. Yet power is also the means by which we bring life, create possibilities, offer hope and make human flourishing possible.

With his trademark clear-headed analysis, Andy Crouch unpacks the dynamics of power that either can make flourishing possible or can destroy the image of God in people. While the effects of power are often evident, he uncovers why power is frequently hidden. He considers not just its personal side but the ways power resides in institutions.

Throughout Crouch offers fresh insights from key biblical passages, demonstrating how Scripture calls us to discipline our power. Wielding power need not distort us or others, but instead can be stewarded well.

An essential book for all who would influence their world for the good.

> *"Once again, Andy Crouch cuts to the heart of the matter by challenging us to take seriously the One whose image we bear.* Playing God *is a clear and compelling call for Christians to steward the kind of power that enables flourishing."*
>
> **Gabe Lyons, coauthor of *unChristian***

ABOUT THE AUTHOR: Andy Crouch is executive editor of *Christianity Today*, where he was also executive producer of This Is Our City, a multiyear project featuring documentary video, reporting and essays about Christians seeking the flourishing of their cities.

Watch six short videos of Andy at ivpress.com/playinggod.

◆ QUESTIONS

1. The author says power is a gift (p. 9). Why do most people have a hard time thinking that power is good?

2. Which vision of reality do you find more appealing or true to life—Nietzsche's will to power or Crouch's creating to flourish (p. 51)?

3. On the author's train trip with Jayakumar Christian, the director of World Vision India said, "The poor are poor because someone else is trying to play God in their lives" (p. 68). What is meant by this phrase?

4. Crouch writes, "God hates injustice and idolatry because they are the same thing" (p. 71). Do you agree or disagree with this statement? Why?

5. Looking at chapter 6, "The Hiddenness of Power," why is power so often invisible to those who have it?

6. In chapter 8 Crouch says privilege is the ongoing benefit we receive from past successful acts of power, like being understood around the world because we happened to grow up speaking English or never being randomly stopped by police because of the color of our skin. The benefits of privilege are pretty self-evident. What are the dangers?

7. Zombie institutions are those that don't create power and flourishing but leach them from society. Crouch suggests in chapter 10 that zombie churches exist to keep the lights on rather than to be the light in dark places. How would you evaluate your own church on the following scale? Explain your answer.

1	2	3	4	5	6	7	8	9	10
Corpse				Zombie			Life-Giving Body		

8. In chapter 12 the author suggests that the classic spiritual disciplines can help us discipline our use of power. How can such disciplines lead us away from power and toward humility?

9. In chapter 13 we read about the Old Testament practice of gleaning, leaving the edges of fields unharvested for those in need to gather for themselves instead of the powerful and privileged keeping everything that is "rightfully" theirs. What are some practical ways we could give others opportunities so they can flourish?

POPCULTURED
Thinking Christianly About Style, Media and Entertainment

Steve Turner

There's no avoiding popular culture—we've been enculturated into it. What does it mean to be faithful Christians in a pop-culture world?

Steve Turner has spent his career chronicling and interviewing people from the worlds of music, film, television, fashion, art and literature. Now he provides an insider's guide to a wide range of pop-culture genres through a Christian framework. Turner explores

- how movies use redemptive narratives and parables
- ways journalistic headlines convey worldview assumptions
- differences between famous people in the past and celebrities today
- how technology changes our sense of what is real

This book will help you become a better cultural critic, consumer and creator.

> *"Steve Turner has proved himself one of the most accessible writers on the interaction of faith and culture. Popcultured is a welcome and lively exploration of what is fast becoming a crucial field."*
>
> **Jeremy Begbie, Duke University, author of *Resounding Truth: Christian Wisdom in the World of Music***

ABOUT THE AUTHOR: Steve Turner is a writer and poet living in London, England, where he regularly contributes to newspapers such as *The Mail on Sunday* and *The Times*. His many books include *Conversations with Eric Clapton, U2: Rattle and Hum, Van Morrison: Too Late to Stop Now* and *A Hard Day's Write: The Stories Behind Every Beatles Song.*

INTERVARSITY PRESS

◆ QUESTIONS

1. What is the most significant form of popular culture in your life?

2. Can you think of attempts by Christians to use popular culture that have left you feeling embarrassed?

3. How do you distinguish between much-needed relaxation and wasting time?

4. What movie has been genuinely prophetic in that it pointed out a flaw in society and challenged viewers to behave differently?

5. To what extent does the media set the agenda for what people consider to be the important issues in their culture?

6. In what way can fame be seen as a secular form of salvation?

7. What does the increasing acceptance of nudity tell us about our culture?

8. Why do we buy designer clothing?

9. What are your favorite methods for coping with boredom?

10. Do you think people ever use manufactured excitement and nonstop entertainment to avoid confronting the big questions of life?

11. If it's true that comedy reveals what we cherish and what we despise, what do you think contemporary comedy tells us about the values of our society?

12. Describe an ad that attracted or repelled you. What caused that particular reaction?

13. Does social networking make you more or less honest with your "friends"?

14. Think of two ways the Internet has helped improve your spiritual life and two ways it has damaged it.

15. If Jesus had owned a camera, what are some of the things he might have photographed?

16. What one change will you make in your consumption of pop culture?

What initially made you interested in studying the relationship between religion and culture?

Stever Turner: It's the story of my life. My parents, who were both from nonreligious families, became Christians around the time I was born, so I grew up in a strong and enthusiastic Christian home. At the same time I was hearing these other voices coming from pop culture, especially in my teenage years, and it became important for me to understand each source of information in light of the other. I needed to know how the values and views found in pop culture could be tested against the Bible and Christian theology, and how ideas from the Bible and Christian theology could stick up for themselves in popular culture. I'm still doing this!

How has your career as a journalist shaped the way you view arts and culture?

Steve: All my writing—as a journalist, author and poet—has helped me understand the creative process. It has helped me identify with creative people. At the same time it has enabled me to have a front-row seat at many important cultural events and given me access to the people who make the culture. I count it as a great privilege to have been able to sit down with many culture makers and ask them how and why they do what they do.

You write that "popular culture constantly veers between authentic personal expression and commercial exploitation." How do you find the balance? And what combination of those two makes popular culture meaningful?

Steve: I don't think it's a case of finding a balance. There's nothing wrong with a toe-tapping tune and there's nothing wrong with a deeply confessional poem. Each has its place. Ecclesiastes 3:4 says that there's a time to dance and a time to mourn. If someone is exclusively into one or the other you might suggest that they try something new, but generally it's good to find pop culture that helps us relax and good to find pop culture that helps us think. I think it's a great achievement when pop culture manages to be both greatly entertaining and profoundly thoughtful at the same time. This happens with some of George Carlin's comedy, a musical like *Les Misérables*, a film like *Amadeus* and the songs of the Beatles.

Who has been your favorite creator of popular culture that you've worked with personally? Why?

Steve: I suppose John Lennon and Paul McCartney. I interviewed John when I was quite young, and it was significant because he had loomed so large in my teenage imagination. I liked his way with words, the risks he took with his work and the fact that he constantly challenged received opinion. I've also interviewed Paul, but because I was the ghostwriter on Linda McCartney's book of sixties photos I got to know him much better. I had breakfast with him at his home in Sussex and he would sometimes sit in on my interviews with Linda and throw in some of his own memories.

What is the number-one idea you want readers to take away from *Popcultured*?

Steve: That it's possible to understand pop culture using a biblically informed mind and that this doesn't lessen the appreciation but increases it. I used to think that if you started to think about culture Christianly it would either adversely affect your faith or adversely affect your enjoyment of culture. Now I see that it can make your faith more robust and useful and can also deepen your love of culture. We make culture because we are made by God, and however defiant and atheistic people are they cannot shake off the divine image. I would like the book to lead Christians in confidently contributing to the ongoing discussions about culture and within culture.

RECONCILING ALL THINGS
A Christian Voice for Justice, Peace and Healing

Emmanuel Katongole and Chris Rice

Our world is broken and cries out for reconciliation.

What makes real reconciliation possible? How is it that some people are able to forgive the most horrendous of evils? And what role does God play in these stories?

In *Reconciling All Things* Emmanuel Katongole and Chris Rice cast a comprehensive vision for reconciliation that is biblical, transformative, holistic and global.

"My only concern is that not enough people will read this fine book! Given how much humans let things fall apart, this resource is a gem for individuals, groups and institutions."

Richard Rohr, O.F.M., Center for Action and Contemplation, Albuquerque, New Mexico

"Read it and heed the call to join in God's great story of reconciliation. You will find yourself challenged beyond comfort, yet moved with great expectations."

Leighton Ford, president, Leighton Ford Ministries, author, *Transforming Leadership* and *The Attentive Life*

ABOUT THE AUTHORS: Emmanuel Katongole (Ph.D., Catholic University of Louvain) grew up in Uganda, was ordained a Catholic priest of Kampala diocese, and has taught at the Uganda National Seminary and Duke Divinity School. He is associate professor of theology and peace studies at the University of Notre Dame.

Chris Rice (M.Div., Duke Divinity School) spent many years living and working in Jackson, Mississippi, with Voice of Calvary Ministries.

Katongole and Rice are founding codirectors of the Center for Reconciliation at Duke Divinity School.

INTERVARSITY PRESS

◆ QUESTIONS

1. Chris and Emmanuel come to learn that "the church's brokenness was at the heart of our restlessness" (p. 16). What makes you restless? How is the church broken?

2. What do you think of when you hear the word *reconciliation*?

3. The authors list four models of reconciliation that they find lacking in some way. Do you agree?

4. What does 2 Corinthians 5:17-19 tell us about both God's role and our role in reconciliation?

5. On pages 43 and 44 the authors describe reconciliation as a gift. What does this mean?

6. Chris describes his own conversion from desiring to be a "fixer" to seeing his need to be changed and taught by the very people he desired to "fix." Can you relate?

7. What is the difference between "peaceful coexistence" and "new creation"?

8. The authors suggest that speeding through the journey of reconciliation can mask "the true depth of trauma in our world" (p. 82). Why is lament necessary?

9. Why are both "prophetic presence" and "prophetic distance" necessary?

10. How does reconciliation take place in "the small, the weak and the ordinary"?

11. What does it mean for the church to point beyond itself (p. 113)?

12. The authors suggest that Christian leadership is about seeing and responding to a "gap." What does it mean to "belong to the gap"?

13. What do we learn from Archbishop Odama about the importance of belonging to God?

14. The authors end the book with ten theses for recovering reconciliation as the mission of God. Which comes to you as particularly good news?

15. How will you move forward in your journey of reconciliation?

What is the purpose of the Center for Reconciliation, and how is that accomplished?

Emmanuel Katongole and Chris Rice: Founded in 2005 and rooted in a Christian vision of God's mission, the Center for Reconciliation at Duke Divinity School inspires, forms and supports leaders, communities and congregations to live as ambassadors of reconciliation.

The Center pursues three strategic goals: cultivating new leaders; communicating wisdom, insights, hopes and practices; and connecting in partnership to strengthen leaders across the world. Programs include serving U.S. leaders through study weeks, workshops and institutes; an African Great Lakes Initiative serving leaders in Uganda, southern Sudan, eastern Congo, Rwanda, Burundi and Kenya; in-depth formation through residential programs at Duke Divinity School; student apprenticeships in exemplary communities of practice; and the Resources for Reconciliation book series.

How did Resources for Reconciliation come about?

Emmanuel and Chris: Through the journeys of the Center's codirectors throughout the world, we learned that one of the greatest needs is fresh literature to help Christians live well in a broken world. Second Corinthians 5 testifies that through Christ, the message of reconciliation has been entrusted to us—the church. Yet the Christian community has largely not taken up this challenge. In conflicts such as the Rwandan genocide and challenges such as family fragmentation, neglected neighborhoods, urban violence, the mentally and physically disabled, and ongoing racial and ethnic divisions in America and worldwide, the church has typically mirrored society rather than offering a witness to it. Yet wherever we go in the most broken places of the world, God is always planting seeds of hope. Resources for Reconciliation is about offering hope for Christians to live well in a broken world by offering fresh stories and practical wisdom to help Christians live faithfully.

InterVarsity Press

What are these resources for?

Emmanuel and Chris: These books provide fresh stories and practices to help Christians live well in a broken world. Their mix of theological vision, stories of hope and practical wisdom is unique.

How does the first book, *Reconciling All Things,* set the tone for the rest of the books in the series?

Emmanuel and Chris: The quest of everyday people for God's new creation in a broken world is the theme of the Resources for Reconciliation book series. In *Reconciling All Things* Chris Rice speaks from his journey in the U.S. and Emmanuel Katongole from his journey in Africa to cast a broad and practical vision for reconciliation which is centered in Christ. The book traces the broad strokes of a journey of reconciliation that is distinctly Christian—a movement from seeing the story of Scripture, to learning to lament, to seeing what hope looks like in a broken world, to drawing from the stories of Christian witnesses for hope from their work with the disabled, to racial reconciliation, to historical conflicts, to family brokenness. The following books in the series will dive into specific contexts of brokenness, to see what hope looks like in the brokenness, such as families, the poor, the disabled, racial and ethnic divisions, the environment, and religious divides such as between Islam and Christianity.

What is your hope for Resources for Reconciliation?

Emmanuel and Chris: To inspire Christians to see that reconciliation is a central part of their journey with Christ. How? By putting fresh and exciting books out over the next few years written by leading practitioners and theologians which will illuminate what hope looks like and how to pursue reconciliation in real places, from congregations to communities.

SENSIBLE SHOES

A Story About The Spiritual Journey

Sharon Garlough Brown

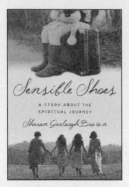

Sharon Garlough Brown tells the moving story of four strangers as they embark together on a journey of spiritual formation:

Hannah, a pastor who doesn't realize how exhausted she is.

Meg, a widow and recent empty nester who is haunted by her past.

Mara, a woman who has experienced a lifetime of rejection and is now trying to navigate a difficult marriage.

Charissa, a hard-working graduate student who wants to get things right.

Join them as they reluctantly arrive at a retreat center and find themselves drawn out of their separate stories of struggle and into a journey of mutual support and personal revelation.

> *"Sharon Garlough Brown introduces us to four engaging women who are wrestling with their . . . view of God. Strap on your best traveling shoes—following their journey in* Sensible Shoes *is not for the faint of heart!"*
>
> **Melinda Correa Schmidt,** *Midday Connection*

> *"If you're a spiritually inclined person, I think you'll really love it. It's about four women, every one of them coming from a different place spiritually. But all of them in need of a [new] fresh cup of mercy. . . . I highly recommend it."*
>
> **Kathie Lee Gifford, NBC's** *Today,* **March 11, 2013**

ABOUT THE AUTHOR: Sharon Garlough Brown holds an M.Div. from Princeton Theological Seminary and is a pastor and spiritual director with the Evangelical Covenant Church. She lives in West Michigan with her husband, Jack, and son, David.

INTERVARSITY PRESS

◆ QUESTIONS

1. If you could sit and have a conversation with one of the characters (Hannah, Meg, Mara and Charissa), who would you choose? Why? What would you want to talk about?

2. Which character did you most identify with? Least identify? Did your opinion change as the story unfolded?

3. Think about the childhood experiences for each character. How did these events shape each woman's sense of identity?

4. Identify turning points for the main characters. Why were these moments significant?

5. What are some of the important growth points or unresolved issues for each character? What next steps do you hope each one takes?

6. Mara says, "I hate the word *discipline*. I already feel guilty." What is your reaction to the concept of spiritual disciplines?

7. How do you define "spiritual formation"?

8. What do you find either appealing or frightening about taking a sacred journey with other people?

9. Dr. Allen says, "The things that annoy, irritate and disappoint us have just as much power to reveal the truth about ourselves as anything else. Learn to linger with what provokes you. You may just find the Spirit of God moving there." What provoked you as you read the book?

10. Meg says, "It's easy to lose sight of how far I've come if I'm only looking at how far I have to go." When do you feel overwhelmed or discouraged by the distance you still have to travel? What helps you keep a God-ward perspective on your journey?

11. How would you respond to an invitation from New Hope?

12. What is God stirring in you as a result of reading this book?

Conversation with . . . **Sharon Garlough Brown**

What is the story behind *Sensible Shoes*?

Sharon Garlough Brown: In September of 2008 I began leading a weekly women's spiritual formation group at the church where my husband and I pastor. I had led many kinds of groups over the years—Bible studies, prayer groups, pastoral care groups and book discussions—and I thought I knew what this Monday morning group of twelve women would become. I expected to study spiritual disciplines together, using one of the many excellent resources about how Christ is formed in us.

By our second meeting, however, I was convinced that God was asking me to drop the idea of a book study. Instead, he was inviting me to trust him to journey into an unknown place without a syllabus or a curriculum. I began to introduce to the group some of the spiritual disciplines that had been life-giving to me: *lectio divina*, the prayer of examen, the labyrinth, journaling, spiritual direction and contemplative prayer. We learned to sit with stillness and silence. Our time together became sacred space where we encountered the living God. The women grew to deeply trust one another, confessing their sins and heartaches so that they could be more open to receiving God's healing love and power.

In one of our first meetings together, one of the women in the group looked around the circle, commenting, "Everybody here is wearing really cute but sensible shoes!" The phrase stuck, and we began to refer to ourselves as the "Sensible Shoes Club." God was leading us through the difficult, unpredictable and sometimes treacherous terrain of the inner life, and we needed sensible shoes for the journey. We also needed one another.

As we walked together, we began to witness stunning and breathtakingly beautiful transformation. The Spirit was healing old wounds, opening blind eyes and setting captives free. I began to sense that God was inviting me to share the story of the group by creating characters who were also learning to walk closely with God. And so, Meg, Hannah, Mara and Charissa emerged from my imagination, surprising me with their own stories of struggle and grace. None of the characters represent "real" people. But they do wrestle with real issues: letting go of control, trusting God, people-pleasing, perfectionism, hiding behind roles and busyness, fear, regret, guilt and shame. Though the details are different, their stories are our stories of healing and redemption.

 InterVarsity Press

What is the main message that comes out of *Sensible Shoes*?

Sharon: We are extravagantly loved by God, and we are called to walk together in that love. God invites us to explore the ways we have hidden from him, others and ourselves so that we can experience healing, transformation and freedom.

How is this book different than other books on spiritual formation?

Sharon: The use of fiction to present spiritual disciplines is a unique approach and provides a gentle entry point for readers who have never heard of spiritual formation. The book gives language to express longings for deeper intimacy with God. The characters serve as windows and mirrors for seeing God and ourselves more clearly. We find our stories in their stories.

What do you hope readers take away from *Sensible Shoes*?

Sharon: Confidence in the lavish love of God. Courage to pursue healing and transformation. Longing for authentic Christian community. Desire to explore spiritual formation, especially to explore spiritual disciplines not as obligations or guilt-driven burdens but as ways to practice receiving, resting in and responding to the love of God. Insights about our own patterns of resisting and avoiding intimacy with God, self and others

THE SINGER

A Classic Retelling of Cosmic Conflict

25th Anniversary Edition

Calvin Miller

The Singer quickly became a favorite of evangelists, pastors, artists, students, teachers and readers of all sorts when it was originally published in 1975. Retelling the story of Christ through an allegorical and poetic narrative of a Singer whose Song could not be silenced, Miller's work reinvigorated Christian literature and offered believers and seekers the world over a deeply personal encounter with the gospel.

Now available in hardcover for the first time in many years, this edition features a new cover illustration by Jerry Tiritilli to complement the classic interior illustrations by Joe DeVelasco. Miller also includes a new preface in which he reveals how he came to write *The Singer* and how he, like so many other readers, has been transformed by its imaginative power.

"*The Singer was a groundbreaking book, and I'm delighted to see its reintroduction.*"

Philip Yancey, author of *The Jesus I Never Knew*

ABOUT THE AUTHOR: Calvin Miller (1936-2012) was a professor at Beeson Divinity School. The beloved author of more than forty books, Miller was also well known as a poet, artist, novelist and speaker. His later works included *Preaching* (Baker), *O Shepherd Where Art Thou?* (Broadman & Holman) and *Conversations with Jesus* (Harvest House). He summed up his rule of life in four words: "Time is a gift."

◆ QUESTIONS

1. *The Singer* is written in the form of an allegorical poem. In what ways does the form illuminate, for you, its message to a greater—or lesser—degree than if the story were told in traditional novel form?

2. Throughout the book, Calvin Miller changes the characters' names. Why might he have done that?

3. What made the Miller with the gnarled hand (pp. 74-77) reject the Singer's offer of healing power within the Melody of the Song? Have you ever rejected a gift you longed to accept? If so, why?

4. Why do you think Calvin Miller used epigraphs within *The Singer*? Did you have a favorite?

5. How did you respond to Calvin Miller's portrayal of World Hater on the one hand and the Singer on the other?

6. *The Singer* is said to be an artful retelling of portions of the four gospels in the New Testament. In what ways did the book amplify—or confuse—the stories you've read or heard from the gospels?

7. What was it in the Singer's song that allowed the Madman to be "entirely at peace" (p. 90). after encountering the Troubadour?

8. "Earthmaker leaves the scars, for they preserve the memory of pain," the Singer tells the child who implores him to heal his own feet and hands, just as he had healed hers (p. 142). "He will leave my hands this way so men will not forget what it can cost to be a singer in a theater of hate." How do you respond to the thought that Earthmaker chose to leave the Singer's hands scarred?

9. What were your emotions in the closing portion of the text, as the Madman once again "strained against his chains" only to find them unlocking themselves and falling away at the sound of the Singer's song?

He was not alone when he awoke.
The ancient World Hater had
come upon his resting place
and not by chance.

The Hater leered at him with
one defiant, impish grin.

"Hello, Singer!"

"Hello, World Hater," the
Troubadour responded.

"You know me by name, old friend
of man?"

"As you know mine, old enemy of
God."

"What brings you to the desert?"

"The Giver of the Song!"

"And does he let you sing it
only in these isolated spots?"

"I only practice here to sing it
in the crowded ways!"

It was hard to sing before the
World Hater, for he ground each
joyous stanza underneath his heel.

The music only seemed to make
the venom in his hate more
bitter than before.

INTERVARSITY PRESS

SURRENDER TO LOVE

Discovering the Heart of Christian Spirituality

David G. Benner

In our self-reliant era, most of us recoil from the concept of surrendering to a power or authority outside ourselves. But surrender need not be seen as threatening, especially when the One to whom we surrender is the epitome of love.

In this profound book, David Benner explores the twin themes of love and surrender as the heart of Christian spirituality. Through careful examination of Scripture and reflection on the Christian tradition, Benner shows how God bids us to trust fully in his perfect love. In each chapter he includes meditative exercises to guide you into a greater experience of trust and spiritual transformation.

Surrender to Love will lead you to an unexpected place, where yieldedness to God frees you to become who he created you to be.

> *"This is one of the most beautiful, powerful and insightful books I have ever read. Dr. Benner shares his lived experience in a way that opens for the reader the possibility of a true transformation."*
>
> **M. Basil Pennington, O.C.S.O., abbot, Abbey of Blessed Mary of Saint Joseph, and author of *Centering Prayer***

ABOUT THE AUTHOR: David G. Benner is Emeritus Distinguished Professor of Psychology and Spirituality at Richmont Graduate University in Atlanta, Georgia. A depth psychologist, spiritual director and retreat leader, Benner has written and edited many books, including the *Baker Encyclopedia of Psychology and Counseling* and *Care of Souls*. He is the founding executive editor of the journal *Conversations*.

INTERVARSITY PRESS

◆ QUESTIONS

1. The idea of surrender is frightening to some people. Before you began this book where did you fall on the surrender scale?

   Surrender — — — — — — —— Never Surrender

2. What similarities or differences do you find between surrender and submission, obedience, love and spirituality?

3. When the author posed the question "What do you assume God feels when you come to mind?" (p. 15), it often elicited answers of disappointment or anger. Did that surprise you? What was your response?

4. Benner calls Christianity the world's greatest love religion and the act of creation a love story. He says, "Human beings exist because of God's desire for companionship" (p. 23). Do you agree with Benner? How does this affect your understanding of Genesis?

5. One of the things that prevents us from dealing with our fear is that most of us don't think of ourselves as fearful. Benner gives several examples of how fear lurks in our life. Where have you become aware of the presence of fear in your life? Is there a verse or passage from the end of the chapter that was helpful?

6. Benner challenges the practice of obedience through sheer will power. Instead he points us to surrender. Where does your ability to obey God come from? Is the idea of surrender more palatable than obedience?

7. Why might encounters with God's love not have transforming consequences?

8. Angie's reaction to the word *surrender* changed throughout the course of the book. How has yours changed?

9. How does a growth in love cause a shift from "focus on me" to an awareness of others?

10. Does the explanation of threefold conversion (p. 98-100) help you understand the place of crisis in our spiritual formation?

11. What has Benner said to convince you that God is head-over-heels in love with you?

TABLE IN THE DARKNESS

A Healing Journey Through an Eating Disorder

Lee Wolfe Blum

"I stood in front of the full-length mirror in my dorm room and inspected the extra parts. These extra parts needed fixing—my stomach, my thighs, and those cheeks that were round and puffy, like two big apples on the side of my face. I would fix this. Fixing was my forte."

These were the thoughts that plagued Lee Blum during her teens and into her twenties. They drove her to an eating disorder and exercise addiction. Eventually, she found herself hospitalized with clinical depression.

But that's not the end of the story: drawing strength from psychological, physiological and spiritual sources, she found her voice again. If you or someone you love has been at this dark table, you will find her story enlightening and encouraging.

"Having waged my own war with eating disorders, I identified with Lee's account of almost overwhelming struggles, and then the welcome outcome of a hard-won recovery. Her story is raw, real and revealing, . . . a clear and victorious validation of the fact that recovery is possible."

Cherry Boone O'Neill, author of *Starving for Attention*, eldest daughter of Pat Boone

ABOUT THE AUTHOR: Lee Wolfe Blum is a health educator at the Melrose Center for Eating Disorders in Minnesota. She works on the Eating Disorders Chemical Dependency team helping those who struggle with this dual diagnosis find hope and freedom. Lee also runs recovery workshops that inspire patients using the gifts she has gained through her own recovery.

Connect with Lee at leewolfeblum.com

InterVarsity Press

◆ QUESTIONS

1. How does the cover of *Table in the Darkness* relate to the content? What emotions does it convey?

2. What factors do you think contributed to Lee's eating disorder? Could it have been avoided, or was it inevitable?

3. Lee writes on page 46 about an interaction with her mom's friend Ron, "I bit my tongue when really I wanted to lash him." How do you think situations like this contributed to Lee's eating disorder?

4. Do you think Lee's primary fear was getting fat, or was she afraid of something else? If something else, what was it?

5. When Lee tells Chris about her eating disorder, she expects him to run. When he doesn't, she asks herself, "Is this how God sees me too?" (p. 82). In what ways does Lee's relationship with Chris begin to influence her view of God?

6. After leaving Menninger, Lee convinced herself that she didn't need anyone's help (p. 129). Why do you think she felt the need to make her way alone rather than asking for help?

7. On page 144 Lee writes, "Eating disorders are not choices, but recovery is." Explain what you think she means. After reading Lee's book, how has your understanding of eating disorders and depression changed, if at all?

8. The woman who Lee stayed with after she first got out of the hospital ended up asking her to leave. What do you think she was afraid of?

9. What are the seven keys Lee describes at the end of the book that are necessary for recovery? How do you see those reflected in her story?

10. Do you know anyone who has wrestled with depression or an eating disorder? After reading Lee's story, what would you say or not say to someone struggling?

11. What role do you think the Christian community played in Lee's recovery? What do you think they did that helped her the most? What could they have done differently to help her?

Conversation with . . . Lee Wolfe Blum

Table in the Darkness **is largely about your personal struggle with depression and an eating disorder. What made you want to uncover all of that anguish very publicly in a book?**

Lee Wolfe Blum: I wrote this book because when I was in treatment I never met another person or heard of anyone who had ever lived life on the other side of an eating disorder. The same is true with the patients I work with, they long to know someone who has recovered, and when I tell them I have, they are so grateful.

What made it so difficult to find mental, physical and spiritual restoration, particularly as a Christian?

Lee: My Christian friends were telling me to pray it away, and the medical community was telling me that I would always struggle in some way. It was confusing and depressing. I want people to read this story and know that God does heal and we have to do the work in recovery. I wrote this because I want people to know that you can live life on the other side of recovery. I also wrote it so people can understand how eating disorders happen, how they aren't a choice and parents don't "cause" eating disorders, but recovery is a choice. And really, the main reason I wrote the book is to offer hope!

Is there some part of you that says, as Christians this isn't something we should be struggling with?

Lee: Being a Christian does not make you immune to struggling with addiction, an eating disorder or depression, and just telling someone to pray will not heal them. But the reach of this book is anyone who is grappling with the question, "Am I good enough?" Of course recovery isn't as simple as one Bible verse or one prayer. But recovery is possible.

You currently work as a health educator at an eating disorder institute. What gives you the strength to help such hurting people each day?

Lee: My passion for this book comes every day when I look in their eyes—those begging for hope, trapped in dark places, sucked in by a disease. I work at a hospital for patients with eating disorders, and I speak to thousands every year at conferences, churches and schools. And it is in the eyes that I find the passion for this book.

InterVarsity Press

Daily I walk through the trenches of those who are in the darkness that I was once in and hold the hands of those who are willing to enter into the freedom that can only be found in God's amazing, awesome and overwhelming love while also doing the work they need to do for recovery.

What do you hope readers, both those who are struggling with eating disorders and those who are not, take away from *Table in the Darkness*?

Lee:

- Find tremendous insight, inspiration and hope for those struggling with eating disorders or any other type of addiction.
- Learn they are not alone in their obsession for perfection or their desire to "be good enough."
- Learn why addressing this issue sooner rather than later is vital to one's physical, mental, emotional and spiritual health.
- Learn practical tools for walking victoriously out of this disorder.
- Come to understand that while eating disorders are complex diseases, recovery is possible.

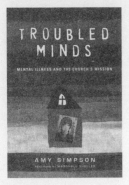

TROUBLED MINDS

Mental Illness and the Church's Mission

Amy Simpson

Foreword by Marshall Shelley

Mental illness is the sort of thing we don't like to talk about. Too often we reduce people who are mentally ill to caricatures and ghosts, and simply pretend they don't exist. They do exist, however—statistics suggest that one in four people suffer from some kind of mental illness. Many of these people are sitting in churches week after week, suffering in stigmatized silence.

In *Troubled Minds* Amy Simpson, whose family knows the trauma and bewilderment of mental illness, reminds us that people with mental illness are our neighbors and our brothers and sisters in Christ, and she shows us the path to loving them well.

"Get ready! Amy Simpson takes you on a thoughtful, vulnerable and even painful journey through the complex landscape of mental illness. There is hope, but not until you go to the emotional and textured depths Troubled Minds *provides."*

John Ortberg, senior pastor, Menlo Park Presbyterian Church

ABOUT THE AUTHOR: Amy Simpson is currently editor of GiftedForLeadership.com and managing editor of marriage and parenting resources for *Today's Christian Woman*. She is formerly vice president, publisher, editor and director of the church ministry media group at Christianity Today.

View video with Amy at ivpress.com/troubledminds.

◆ QUESTIONS

1. The author claims we have a responsibility to intentionally love and help people affected by mental illness, and that is essential to the fulfillment of the church's mission (pp. 31-32). Why would this kind of ministry be core to God's purpose for the church?

2. As the author describes her experience with her mother at the dentist's office in chapter 1 (p. 25), she points out, "And not one person asked me—a completely rational and nonthreatening fifteen-year-old kid—if I needed help." Why do you think no one offered to help?

3. According to the book, why does the author call mental illness "mainstream" (chapter 2)?

4. What surprised you about the author's description of the mental health care system (chapter 4, pp. 81-87)?

5. In chapter 5 (pp. 103-4), Simpson claims many churches simply don't allow messes within their congregations. She says, "Ministering to people with mental illness requires us to get closer to them than—let's be honest—many of us would like to get." Explain how this statement rings true or false with your own experience.

6. Toward the end of chapter 6 (p. 131) how would you answer Simpson's question: "If counselors, social workers and psychiatrists are well equipped to treat people with mental illness and to help them manage and even heal, why is people's experience in the church so important?"

7. How does chapter 7's brief history of the treatment of mental illness in Western civilization (pp. 136-44) inform your understanding of the ways we currently handle mental illness?

8. Chapter 7 points out, "Most of popular media treats the mentally ill as either frightening or funny or both" (p. 144). What examples have you noticed?

9. In chapter 9, Simpson encourages us to consider Christ's redemptive work, both now and in the new life to come (p. 201). How does this redemptive work influence your view of mental illness?

UNDONE

When Coming Apart Puts You Back Together

Laura Sumner Truax

Whether a big crisis shakes us or little things wear away at us, these are moments in which we are confronted with ourselves. This is not the way that things are supposed to be. We feel like failures. Worse yet, we realize that underneath our masks and facades, we are not the people we are pretending to be.

Laura Truax knows what it's like when life hits the fan. But she discovered that these times of exposure and vulnerability can become opportunities to find out who we really are and what we are meant to be. When we come to the end of ourselves, God can meet us there to help us face our fears, take off our masks and rediscover our true self as part of his larger story.

> "[Laura Truax] speaks to those of us still working it all out. She reminds us that we've all been undone and points to us the wholeness that can be found in God's unquenchable love."
>
> **Rob Acton, executive director, Taproot Foundation, NYC**
>
> "In this book Laura Sumner Truax encourages us to embrace these mistakes, disappointments and difficulties as the place where we begin to discover who we really are as beloved children of God."
>
> **Mark Scandrette, author of *Free* and *Practicing the Way of Jesus***

ABOUT THE AUTHOR: Laura Sumner Truax is senior pastor of LaSalle Street Church in Chicago, Illinois. She holds degrees in divinity, pastoral studies and spirituality from Loyola University Divinity School and serves as a teaching pastor for World Vision and for the University of Chicago Divinity School. She and her family live in Chicago.

INTERVARSITY PRESS

◆ QUESTIONS

1. Laura talks about the experience of becoming undone, saying it was both the worst and best day of her life. Was there ever a loss or failure in your life that elicited a sense of relief?

2. Have you ever felt truly at home, at a place where you were loved and valued and supported no matter what? How can you create that sort of environment for others?

3. What are some of the masks you wear? What are the fears that led to that mask's construction?

4. Have you had moments in your life where your "little steps of faith" have led to unexpectedly large results?

5. Consider Laura's statement that change will not occur "until the pain of staying as you are is greater than the pain of changing"(p. 113). Do you believe that? Can you identify examples in your own life where that happened?

6. If God isn't watching us like "babysitters on a nanny-cam," how is God watching us? What does this divine connection with us look like?

7. Do you have the in-the-moment confidence of a child? How can childlike living help restore your identity and grow your childlike trust?

8. Laura talks about a group of people gathered at the Jordan River, people coming from all walks of life but united by a single desire: they wanted something better. What "better" do you want? What is at the root of this desire?

9. Laura says the cross runs against the grain of some of our American posturing about independence. Do you agree or disagree? Why?

10. What does it mean to know God believes in you? Is that phrase powerfully liberating to you?

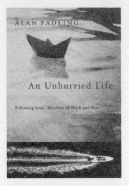

AN UNHURRIED LIFE
Following Jesus' Rhythms of Work and Rest

Alan Fadling

"I am a recovering speed addict."

Beginning with this confession, pastor and spiritual director Alan Fadling goes on to describe his journey out of the fast lane and into the rhythms of Jesus.

Following the framework of Jesus' earthly life, Fadling shows how the work of "unhurrying" ourselves is central to our spiritual development in such pivotal areas as resisting temptation, caring for others, praying and making disciples.

Here is a book that affirms that we are called to work and to do work. Productivity is not a sin; it is the attitudes behind our work that can be our undoing. So how do we find balance between our sense of calling and the call to rest? *An Unhurried Life* offers a way.

> *"Alan Fadling has written a magnificent book that is timely and enduring. It may even become a spiritual classic. . . . As you pick up this book, I urge you to slow, read, savor and be changed in companionship with your unhurried Savior."*
>
> **L. Paul Jensen, executive director of The Leadership Institute**

ABOUT THE AUTHOR: Alan Fadling is executive director of The Journey, a ministry of The Leadership Institute in Orange, California, training Christian leaders to integrate spiritual formation and leadership development.

◆ QUESTIONS

1. How do you respond to the idea of Jesus as relaxed?

2. In what ways do you see busyness in your life—even in your Christian life or ministry life—as more of a hindrance to your following Jesus than a help?

3. Explain how this book's message about unhurriedness could tempt you to justify places of laziness in your thinking, your intentions, or your way of life and work.

4. Which of the three temptations—those related to provision, to authority or honor, or to doubt of God's care—do you find most trouble- some at this stage of your journey? How does Jesus' response to that particular temptation help you here?

5. How does the story of the good Samaritan (Luke 10:30-37) illustrate that being unhurried frees us to show compassion to the person right in front of us?

6. When you hear the word *prayer*, do you feel welcomed in God's presence or guilty for lack of personal faithfulness to such a practice?

7. When do you have times that aren't measured by what you produce, but instead by Sabbath values of relaxation, worship, love and even play?

8. Think about some of the losses you have experienced in your life. Can you now describe them in terms of pruning that produced more or better fruit?

9. If someone asked you, "How do I know if I'm maturing as a follower of Jesus?" what would your response be?

10. When you review some of the practices mentioned in chapter 10 —solitude and silence, unhurried leadership, slowing, sleep, slowness to speak, seeking guidance—which one do you find most attractive? Which seems most challenging?

11. What was your initial response to the idea that we are living eternal life now?

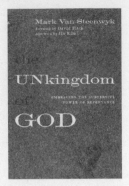

THE UNKINGDOM OF GOD

Embracing the Subversive Power of Repentance

Mark Van Steenwyk
Foreword by David Fitch
Afterword by Jin Kim

Christianity is carrying a lot of baggage. Two thousand years of well-intended (and sometimes not so well-intended) attempts to carry forward the good news of God with us have resulted in some murky understandings of the teachings of Jesus and the culture of God's kingdom. To embrace Christianity, sometimes we have to repent of what we've made of it.

In *The Unkingdom of God* Mark Van Steenwyk explores the various ways we have failed our mission by embracing the ways of the world and advancing our own agendas. He shows us that the starting place of authentic Christian witness is repentance, and that while Jesus' kingdom is not of this world, it remains the only hope of the world.

> "Read at your own risk, but be forewarned—no one gets off easy."
>
> **Carolyn Custis James, author of *Half the Church: Recapturing God's Global Vision for Women***

> "Mark Van Steenwyk is a committed voice of a new generation rising to the ancient calling of radical discipleship."
>
> **Ched Myers, Bartimaeus Cooperative Ministries**

ABOUT THE AUTHOR: Mark Van Steenwyk is cofounder of the Mennonite Worker, a Christian intentional community in Minneapolis. Mark is an editor at JesusRadicals.com and the producer and cohost of the Iconocast podcast.

Watch a video of Mark at ivpress.com/unkingdomofgod.

INTERVARSITY PRESS

◆ QUESTIONS

1. The author writes that "the heart of repentance" is "an invitation to engage the world differently" (p. 16). What appeals to you about this understanding of repentance? What concerns you about it?

2. The author cites the description of Jesus' rulership in Philippians 2: 6-7, with its emphasis on Jesus' humility and servant orientation, and then suggests, "Instead of thinking of Christianity as a superior religion, wouldn't it be better to assert Christianity's inferiority?" (p. 38). Do you agree or disagree? Why?

3. The author draws our attention to the problem of abstraction. "We can care about poverty," he observes, "but not the poor woman on the corner" (p. 45). Where do you observe abstraction getting in the way of a right relation to the world around us?

4. "We think we are open to learning the way of Jesus, but our cup is already full of our own ideas" (p. 76). What does repentance look like when applied to the way we see the world?

5. How do you respond to the author's presentation of "Christian anarchism"? What appeals to you about his vision? Do you have concerns?

6. Which of the author's three practices (pp. 121-25) do you think would be most helpful for you to "rewild" your faith in a "feral God"?

7. The author distinguishes charity from compassion: "Charity," he says, "is the sharing of resources. Compassion is the sharing of life" (p. 133). Charity, the author suggests, often perpetuates injustice, whereas compassion is one of the fruits of our ongoing repentance. How would you describe the interplay of charity and compassion?

8. "Jesus opens for us an economic vision that destroys the economic divisions between people" (p. 160). Jesus is not looking for charity so much as solidarity—an embrace of the poor as brothers and sisters in the family of God. What gets in the way of this solidarity today?

9. "In Jesus' approach, being godly is more about who we include than who we exclude" (p. 169). What are some simple, concrete, practical ways you and your faith community can become more inclusive of the people around you?

WANTING TO BE HER

Body Image Secrets Victoria Won't Tell You

Michelle Graham

How do you feel when you look at a magazine cover?

Do you ever look at the models and wish you looked like them?

Most women have had that experience. When you go to the health club, you notice how buff the woman to the left is and how skinny the woman to the right is. And when you go out, you see the guys flocking to talk with certain women and wonder if your looks stack up to theirs.

In this book Michelle Graham reveals how easy it is to fall into the trap of viewing your body through the lens of culture rather than through the eyes of God. She helps you understand that these are not the things that God wants you to dwell on—nor are they true qualities of beauty.

As you read this book you will discover that beauty comes in all shapes, sizes and colors, and it cannot be airbrushed or faked. In these pages you will discover the true secrets of a positive body image.

> *"My longing for God was reawakened, and my love for other women renewed."*
>
> **Dr. Sarah Sumner, professor of ministry and theology at Azusa Pacific University and author of *Men and Women in the Church***

ABOUT THE AUTHOR: Michelle Graham is a staff member and popular speaker for InterVarsity Christian Fellowship who helps women of all ages develop the courage to live differently in today's culture and to rise up as world changers.

◆ QUESTIONS

1. How do you think the culture has defined beauty?

2. What do you think it was like to be Eve in the garden before sin entered the picture?

3. What stood out to you in the comparisons of shame and grace?

4. What is the secret of contentment? How do we develop a lifestyle of contentment like the apostle Paul?

5. How does the fear of rejection affect your relationships with people?

6. What are some evidences of ethnocentric beauty standards that you have either experienced or witnessed?

7. What stories or facts struck you most in chapter 4? Why? How do you think God feels about these things?

8. How closely do you relate to the young woman in Song of Songs?

9. What would it take for you to respond to beauty standards with the same confidence?

10. What parts of Ezekiel's story were most striking to you? Why?

11. How do you respond to the analogy of prostitution?

12. What has God been teaching you about body obsessions and body neglect?

13. When it comes to modesty, how good are you at being a "secret keeper"?

14. Discuss the difference between looking beautiful and being beautiful. What are some character traits that make a woman beautiful?

15. What connotation does physical beauty have to you? Good? Bad? Shallow? Ultimate? How does that affect the way you view your body?

16. What practices or reminders help you choose to listen to God's opinion instead of the opinion of others?

17. How might acts of loving others and building God's kingdom help you take the focus off yourself?

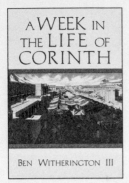

A WEEK IN THE LIFE OF CORINTH

Ben Witherington III

Ben Witherington III attempts to reenchant our reading of Paul in this creative reconstruction of ancient Corinth. Following a fictitious Corinthian man named Nicanor through an eventful week of business dealings and conflict, you will encounter life at various levels of Roman society—eventually meeting Paul himself and gaining entrance into the Christian community there. The result is an unforgettable introduction to life in a major center of the New Testament world. Numerous full-page text boxes expand on a variety of aspects of life and culture as we encounter them in the narrative.

> *"This book provides a uniquely enjoyable way to learn about ancient culture and Paul's mission in Corinth by immersion. Although I found the story delightful and intriguing, I could also see behind it careful research on a large array of details."*
>
> **Craig Keener, author of *1-2 Corinthians* (Cambridge) and *Acts: An Exegetical Commentary* (4 vols.; Baker Academic)**

ABOUT THE AUTHOR: Ben Witherington III (Ph.D., University of Durham, England) is professor of New Testament at Asbury Theological Seminary in Wilmore, Kentucky. He is the author of many books on the New Testament, including *Women and the Genesis of Christianity* (Cambridge University Press), *Jesus the Sage* (Fortress Press), *The Jesus Quest* (InterVarsity Press) and *The Paul Quest* (InterVarsity Press).

◆ QUESTIONS

1. On page 14 Nicanor says that Erastos was part of "a new religious cult in town that met privately only in people's homes." Why was this a secretive and unspoken of topic?

2. How does the image of Paulos in this book, as described at the beginning of chapter 3, contrast or differ from the typical image we perceive of the apostle Paul?

3. Nicanor notes that "some pagan residents had worried that [Christianity] sounded like cannibalism" (p. 34) because they drank the blood and ate the body of Jesus. What else do you imagine would be strange to the early observers outside of Christianity?

4. How does the everyday life of Erastos described in chapter 4 compare with life today?

5. On page 63 it says that Gallio viewed Judaism as being "akin to atheism." Why would this have been a common thought in that time and context?

6. What does the "Closer Look" excerpt on page 102 tell us about Sosthenes complaints against Paulos and what was regarded as an important case in Roman trials?

7. Do you think you would've reacted similarly to Nicanor in response to Erastos being healed by Paul? How would you respond to a miracle like that?

8. On page 148 Nicanor wrestles with the questions he has surrounding the Christian faith, saying that the idea of a god taking the form of a servant and dying on a cross "sounded like foolishness." What do Nicanor's questions and hesitations reveal about religious understandings at this time?

9. What is so powerful about the end of this story and Nicanor's turn of faith in the Christian God? How does it relate to your own experience?

THE WORLD IS NOT OURS TO SAVE

Finding the Freedom to Do Good

Tyler Wigg-Stevenson

We want to save the world—and we have a dizzying array of worthy causes to pursue.

But passionate enthusiasm can quickly give way to disillusionment, compassion fatigue or empty slacktivism. As we move from awareness to mobilization, we bump up against the complexities of global problems—and liking Facebook pages only goes so far.

Veteran activist Tyler Wigg-Stevenson identifies the practical and spiritual pitfalls that threaten much of today's cause-driven Christianity. He casts an alternate vision for doing good based on the liberating truth that only God can save the world.

The world is not ours to save. And that's okay. Discover why.

> *"Tyler's beautifully written essay, theologically penetrating, wise and born out of his own experiences, will give you rest and help you not tire out of radical commitments and faith-based activism."*
>
> **Miroslav Volf, author of *A Public Faith: How Followers of Christ Should Serve the Common Good*, Henry B. Wright Professor of Theology, Yale Divinity School**

ABOUT THE AUTHOR: Tyler Wigg-Stevenson is the founder and director of the Two Futures Project, a movement of Christians for nuclear threat reduction and the global abolition of nuclear weapons. He also serves as chairman of the Global Task Force on Nuclear Weapons for the World Evangelical Alliance.

INTERVARSITY PRESS

◆ QUESTIONS

1. Where do you see Christians doing good in today's culture?

2. Tyler writes that "our heroic impulse also reveals something dark and sinister about human nature" (p. 27). What is the shadow side of heroism? Do you agree with this argument. Why or why not?

3. Tyler calls "sinner's prayer activism" (p. 55) "a bill of goods, at best a half-truth" (p. 59). Do you think Tyler's assessment is fair or not? Have you seen videos like the one described here? How do you tend to react to this kind of appeal?

4. In chapter 4 Tyler suggests that when we are confronted with difficult Bible passages (like Deuteronomy 2:32-36), we pick one of four options: (1) hate God, (2) become monsters, (3) deny that God is really like this or (4) fear God. Have you experienced any of these reactions in your readings of Scripture? How else might you encounter such texts?

5. "We are ourselves the world's most intractable problem" (p. 76). Why does Tyler make this statement? Do you agree with it?

6. Do you think your views on peace are similar to the majority or the minority of other Christians?

7. Tyler describes Coventry Cathedral as a rare exception to the tendency to prioritize evangelism over peace or vice versa. How are evangelism and peace related?

8. Tyler tells the story of DEMDACO as an example of a "plowshares business" (pp. 147-50). What makes this company different? How could this example help transform your own workplace—whether you are the CEO or an intern?

9. In the section on dignity (pp. 163-67) a balance between individual and community welfare is emphasized. Where have you seen this balance succeed (or fail) in your local community?

10. How would Tyler's new vision for Christian activism (pp. 198-203) change your approach to living out your Christianity?

Discussing the book in a group can help clarify any questions readers have as well as sharpen what response is appropriate. The questions for each title assume that participants have read the book. You may want to mention this to your group before you select a book for discussion.

For the leader:

Read the book carefully and mark it up well. Note your own questions or responses.

You don't want to be overbearing, nor do you want to be passive. Your goal is to help the group flourish in its understanding and application of the book, not impress people with how much you know.

In addition to the specific book questions, leaders may also ask questions like, "What parts of this chapter struck you the most? Did you underline or highlight anything that was particularly meaningful to you?"

Additional guidelines to help you:

- At the beginning of your first time together, explain that these studies are meant to be discussions, not lectures. Encourage the members of the group to participate. However, do not put pressure on those who may be hesitant to speak.

- Begin each study on time.

- The study questions are designed to be read aloud just as they are written. You may, however, prefer to express them in your own words.

- Note also that there may be times when it is appropriate to deviate from the discussion guide. For example, a question may have already been answered. If so, move on to the next question. Or someone may raise an important question not covered in the guide. Take time to discuss it, but try to keep the group from going off on tangents.

- Avoid answering your own questions. An eager group quickly becomes passive and silent if members think the leader will do most of the talking. If necessary, repeat or rephrase the question until it is clearly understood, or refer to the commentary woven into the guide to clarify the context or meaning.

- Don't be afraid of silence in response to the discussion questions. People may need time to think about the question before formulating their answers.

- Don't be content with just one answer. Ask, "What do the rest of you think?" or "Anything else?" until several people have given answers to the question.

- Try to be affirming whenever possible. Especially affirm participation. Never reject an answer; if it seems clearly off-base, ask, "What led you to that conclusion?" or again, "What do the rest of you think?"

- Don't expect every answer to be addressed to you, even though this will probably happen at first. As group members become more at ease, they will begin to truly interact with each other. This is one sign of healthy discussion.

- Don't be afraid of controversy. It can be very stimulating. If you don't resolve an issue completely, don't be frustrated. Explain that the group will move on and God may enlighten all of you in later sessions.

- Periodically summarize what the group has said. This helps to draw together the various ideas mentioned and gives continuity to the study. But don't preach.

- End on time.

CONNECT WITH US!

 MORE CONVERSATION STARTERS:
www.ivpress.com/**readup**

BECOME A FAN ON FACEBOOK:
www.facebook.com/**intervarsitypress**

FOLLOW US ON TWITTER:
@ivpress

WATCH US ON YOUTUBE:
www.youtube.com/**intervarsitypress**

FIND US ON GOODREADS:
http://bit.ly/**ivpgoodreads**

READ US ON SCRIBD:
www.scribd.com/**InterVarsityPress**

GET REGULAR UPDATES ON AUTHORS, NEW BOOKS,
SPECIAL DISCOUNTS AND MORE! SIGN UP FOR
ONE OF OUR ENEWSLETTERS:
www.ivpress.com/**newsletters**

INTERVARSITY PRESS